Living *the* Miraculous Life

Beyond the Comfort Zone

by

Bill Dew

Living the Miraculous Life:
Beyond the Comfort Zone

Edited by: Lisa Lindle
        Bob Baynard

Global Awakening
1451 Clark St
Mechanicsburg, PA 17055

Dewnamis Ministries, Inc.
www.dewnamis.com
dewnamis@sbcglobal.net

ENDORSEMENTS

In this amazing account of the early days of renewal, you will be encouraged and challenged by extraordinary testimonies of God's healing power that will leave you on the edge of your seat. "Living the Miraculous Life: Beyond The Comfort Zone" is chock-full of practical insights to effectively help you come to grips with your destiny and begin to fulfill the call of God on your life.

This is one man's journey from being a successful, worldly businessman whose marriage was on the rocks to having an incredible worldwide ministry. Bill's life is a beautiful example of one who has been faithful in the small things and is now entrusted with the great riches of the Kingdom of God.

Gary Oates
Gary Oates Ministries, Inc.
Moravian Falls, NC 28654

If you like good news, you will love this book! Hidden in Bill's engaging personal stories of experiences in the supernatural power of God are nuggets of truth that will help you find your own adventure outside the box of normal. "Living the Miraculous Life: Beyond The Comfort Zone" is a great read for those who are ready for more.

David Crone
Senior Leader
The Mission, Vacaville, CA

Some of the greatest miracles I've seen around the world have been in partnership with Bill and Carol Dew; whenever I am around them, the grace for healing increases in me and all those around us. I believe that this book carries the same anointing to increase your grace and faith for healing, signs and wonders. Bill and Carol are master trainers who present deep spiritual truths in a profoundly simple way.

Dan McCollam
Director of Sounds of the Nations and the Institute for Worship Arts Resources (iWAR)

You've heard the title, "The Greatest Story Ever Told!" This book is a part of that unfolding, never-ending story of God's grace poured out upon a human life. Bill Dew effectively captures the adventure of following God into a destiny of the impossible - one that only God could orchestrate and fulfill. This book will encourage, inspire, and provoke you to the "more" that God has planned for us all.

Bill Johnson
Senior Pastor of Bethel Church, Redding, CA
Author - *When Heaven Invades Earth* & *Face to Face with God*

To my wife, Carol, who kept encouraging me all along the way. 41 years together — like two different marriages, just with the same two people. To my daughter, Trish — the catalyst to my being saved. And to Randy Clark, without whom this wouldn't have been possible. He has many spiritual sons — I'm proud to be one of them.

CONTENTS

FORWARD

"Living the Miraculous Life: Beyond The Comfort Zone" is an example of what can happen to the average person, without previous experience in healing and moving in the Spirit, when they have the opportunity to learn how to move in the gifts. Bill traveled with me for about a year and a half, and I have been amazed by how God has used him and his wife since they launched Dewnamis Ministries. I enjoyed reading Bill's report of what God was doing in our midst during the early days following the outpouring of the Holy Spirit in Toronto. This is reading not a secondary source but a primary source for history of this period. Reading Bill's book, one can learn a lot about how to recognize what the Father is doing, how to flow in the gifts of the Spirit, and how to minister in the heart and spirit of Jesus. The reader can learn, as Bill learned, how to prepare to be used of God with signs following. I congratulate Bill on a great job of both keeping very meticulous notes of that time and of turning those notes into an interesting read that instructs the reader as well as encourages him/her to believe that God can use them also.

Bill and his wife Carol are great teachers, funny, practical, down to earth, biblical, and wise. They have a commitment to help the people in their training events become confident that they can learn to hear from God, step out in faith, and be used by God - not just in the church meetings, but out in the workplace.

As I have traveled around the world and the United States, everyone I have met who have had Bill and Carol in to train for them have had very good reports about their ministry. I am grateful to have had the opportunity to sow into their lives. The seed has truly brought forth a 100 fold harvest.

They are seasoned in ministry and walk in very high integrity in a day when this is becoming more and more important. It truly isn't all about gifting, but also about character. With Bill and Carol you don't have to choose between gifting or character, because they carry both.

Randy Clark, President
Global Awakening, Mechanicsburg, PA
Author - There Is More and Lighting Fires

INTRODUCTION

Since January 20, 1994, there has been renewal that has gone around the world. For me, it started almost two years before in my wife's Presbyterian church. The Holy Spirit landed on me and I was saved, went through further deliverance, and was baptized in the Spirit. I had been a successful businessman but was bound up in a secret sin that I seemed to have no control over. Unfortunately for me, while I believed there was God the Father and I accepted the fact of Jesus, His son, I heard nothing about the power or reality of satan and his demons, or of the Holy Spirit. There might have been some teaching on these subjects, but I didn't **hear** it in the 13 years I attended the church faithfully every Sunday.

For me, the change came dramatically, first sovereignly, and then in partnership with another person praying for me with the laying on of hands. In an encounter with God that lasted nearly three hours, Jesus appeared to me in a vision, told me He loved me, forgave me, and said "and son, you can do this too." I somehow knew that He meant I could move in the power I saw manifested that night. When I finally got up off the floor that night, I knew that I knew that I knew that everything my wife Carol had been trying to tell me was **real**. That night, having never been prayed for until that night, and having never prayed for anyone, for anything, I got to pray for someone who got healed. It was Carol, so I know it was real. From that point on it was like I had been a rocket launched and I began moving in the power of God, especially for physical healing, and I got **desperately** hungry for the things of God.

I didn't know it at the time, but I was the epitome of one man's message, called "God Can Use Little Ole Me." I was the least likely, not qualified spiritually, and nobody knew who I was or what wonderful things God was doing with me. Then, out of nowhere, I got catapulted onto an international stage of ministry – not because of any qualification or striving on my part, but solely through His grace. In His grace, He brought me and my wife through a major crisis in our marriage and gave us a new one. He brought me out from under the spirit of mammon, and He brought me into a place of better understanding His great and incredible love for me. And He continues to bring me into a place of His rest, His trust, and a place of great faith for the impossible.

Having been a history major in college and having seen the biblical principle in action, I know the importance of "telling the testimony." My prayer is that my story will be an encouragement to others. This is not only my story, but also a historical account of the renewal in the middle years. Many times while leading meetings and speaking a message from my heart, I have said "at the end of this, some of you will say 'If God can use **him** and all his insecurities, I **know** He can use me.'" There are incredible adventures waiting for you as you say yes to the Lord and you pursue Him with all your heart. May you be blessed and encouraged by the journey I've been on and continue on even to this day!

CHAPTER 1

STEP OUT OF THE BOAT TO SEE MIRACLES

I was stepping out of the boat, literally. I had heard Randy Clark preach many times from Matthew 14:22-33 about Jesus walking on the water and calling Peter to himself, bidding him to also walk on the water. My wife Carol and I had even taught from this same passage and I had made the statement, "When you step out of the boat, when you leave your comfort zone, you'll see miracles." Now here I was, stepping out of a boat onto a remote island, and I was definitely out of my comfort zone.

"Does everyone have on sandals?" This was the question from one of the Fijian pastors who had driven us out on the boat to a remote island among the many islands of Fiji. This was Saturday the 11th of August, 2001, and it was the last day of a ten day mission trip to Fiji. The Fijian pastor who had arranged for the team to come had asked Dave Crone if he and several others would come out to this island and bless a church that was under construction. Pastor Wagua (pronounced like Wonga), head of the Assemblies of God churches in Fiji, was an apostolic leader in Fiji and the surrounding Pacific Rim. He had developed a relationship with Dave, pastor of Vaca Valley Christian Life Center (now called The Mission) in Vacaville, CA, several years earlier and had invited this team to come to bring the fire of God to the islands. He had been to our church many times and loved the worship, the freedom of the women, and the power of God to change lives, and he wanted this for his leaders and church people. So, on this beautiful Saturday morning, he had sent his wooden boat with two of his pastors to pick up Dave, Bud, Danno, and myself and take us to the island. After all the training and the crusade meetings, the team had gone off to one of the islands to a resort called Musket Cove. The boat was picking us up there, while the rest of the team of 20 was going back to the main island to shop and then rest at the hotel until it was time to go to the airport to catch our flight back to the US.

When Dave asked me if I wanted to go with them, I was instantly in turmoil. I didn't want to go shopping with the rest of the group as they returned to the big island. That shopping always turns into the women going to all those little knick-knack shops. After about the second or third one, they all start to look the same and of course there's not an electronic toy around, no sports equipment, nothing that a guy would be interested in (when I have told this story since, all the ladies in the meeting laugh at me and all the men nod their heads in agreement). On the other hand, I didn't want to go on a boat to a remote island. Even before I thought about the boat we would be traveling on, I was going back and forth about whether to go or not, trying to hear from God what He wanted me to do.

The wind and seas had picked up during the night, and while it was a gorgeous, to-die-for day (thankfully that wasn't a prophetic term!), the seas were the choppiest we had seen them – the first clue that this was not to be an ordinary journey. And then I caught sight of the boat. It was an old wooden boat with a small cabin on it. My first thought was that it seemed very small, not very sea-worthy, and I realized then that I hadn't accurately thought this situation out. When we came over to the resort island, it had been on a large catamaran with a cabin on top, but this was an old, *old* little wooden boat. Nonetheless, there were 20 of the team urging us on, and the other three seemed to think nothing of it, so I tried to relax as I got on board this much smaller boat. Painfully aware of how uncoordinated I felt as I stepped from the dock onto the bobbing boat, I realized right then that I was completely out of my comfort zone. Little did I know just how far out of that zone I was to be taken.

In hindsight, I think I'm grateful I didn't realize this as well: Pastor Waqua **sent** his boat - he didn't even come on this trip. Hmmm.

For the next hour and a half we bounced and bucked on the seas toward an island we knew nothing about, heading into an unknown situation. The only real comfort was that we had two Fijian pastors on board who said they knew what they were doing, and the scenery was absolutely breathtaking. The sea was a mixture of blues and greens, and we passed many remote islands with inviting white sandy beaches. Finally, we came to the island called Ya-Know-Ya (at least that's what it sounded like when they said it).

OK, LET'S GET HONEST

Now, I'm going to be open, transparent, and vulnerable with you so you get the full picture. Dave, Danno, and Bud are rough and tumble, ready for anything bring-on-the-adventure kind of guys – or at least it seemed like that to me. I'm not. I tend to be more fastidious, don't like to get dirty or messed up, the organized, left-brained kind of guy that's thinking that I'm supposed to get on a plane later that night so don't get messed up and what are you doing out here in the first place? As we neared the island, I realized there's no way there's going to be a dock. At least I'm wearing shorts (which is already a stretch for me unless it's tennis shorts) but I'm wearing my loafers and I can't get them wet because I'm wearing them home that night. Now, I could have jumped into the water with my shoes off, and I was preparing to do that when the Fijian pastor asked the question, "Does everyone have on sandals?" Seeing that I didn't, he said "Get on my back and I'll take you to shore." So I rode "piggyback" style on his back to the shore and I'll be forever grateful.

This will give you an idea of how my mind works. I had already reasoned I would jump in the water, get my feet wet, get sandy feet on the beach with no towel to wipe the sand off, and be uncomfortable when I had to put my shoes back on. But by riding "piggyback," I arrived on the beach dry and clean. See how my mind works? Yes, sometimes it's hard to be me.

As several other pastors came to lead us into the heart of the village, I began to get the "we're not in Kansas anymore" picture. The island was dotted with huts and a few small block buildings. There were no roads and no vehicles. Chickens and pigs were everywhere. Many of the people were greeting us, staring as we passed by. I wondered as I looked at the kids if they had ever seen any white people before.

When we met with the pastor of the church we had come to bless, we learned that the island held about 470 people, was almost completely Christian, and those who work do so at a nearby resort. I was struck by the fact that we were now seeing a third Fiji. The first Fiji we were in was not very pretty, no beautiful sandy beaches, lots of poverty, and about half Fijian and half Indian. The second Fiji is the resort Fiji, the one you see on the postcards. It's the one with the thatched roof huts, the beautiful beaches, great restaurants, and endless recreational pastimes like snorkeling and scuba diving. Now we had entered the third Fiji. This is the one of the remote islands accessible only by boat, of no electricity, and very primitive. It was like stepping back in time.

"CAST AWAY" - OH, I HOPE NOT

They first wanted us to see the church that had been under construction for the past three months. The block walls were up with no windows, the sand floor prepared for the concrete to be poured, and roof joists in, but no roof. When finished it would hold about 100 people. As we walked around and admired what had been done so far, we all realized that we were hearing the crashing of waves nearby. It was only then that we noticed a gorgeous sandy beach with waves pounding against it, about 25 yards away from the building. The only thing missing was surfers – it was an incredible setting. Then we saw a beautiful island about 1000 yards out. The pastor told us it was the island that was used in the filming of the movie "Cast Away" with Tom Hanks. We took in the white sandy beach and the high point of the island which held a prominent place in the movie. I suppressed any fear of a re-enactment of the movie, and Dave began to pray and bless the church.

By now there were about 10 Fijians around. When we had first met the pastor we had told of the crusade meetings we had just been in and some of the incredible stories of healings that had occurred. Somehow it came out that he had a pain in his wrist, so I asked if I could pray for him. My wife and I teach about taking the power of God out of the church to wherever we are, so it was a great place to demonstrate it. The pain left almost immediately and he wiggled his wrist all around to test it. Then they told us one of the men had pain in his chest for the past three months and asked if I would pray for him. As I began to pray, his left hand began to shake. Now, at this point in 2001, I had been praying for people since 1992, when I got saved and gloriously baptized in the Spirit. I had ministered around the world, traveled with Randy Clark for 16 months, and had seen a lot, so this shouldn't have shocked me, but I could almost hear the whirring of my little left brain when there was a sudden realization: "They haven't seen the power of God before, they haven't been to the big crusades we've just had, this is no power of suggestion, it's REALLY REAL! Wow." His shaking increased, then down he went into Bud's arms and onto the sand. He didn't do "carpet time." *This* was doing "sand time." He didn't care. He got up several minutes later completely pain free, able to breathe deeply for the first time in months.

YOU CAN CALL IT A SULU, BUT IT'S A SKIRT

We returned to the pastor's house, and they showed us where the women were preparing our lunch outside. The men had gone diving the previous night and had caught enough lobster to feed the whole team of 24. They thought all of us on the team were coming. Not only that, they had fish, crab, and potatoes. We were in for a feast, but first we had to pay a visit to the chief of the island. Apparently nothing gets past the chief. To go see him, you have to wear a traditional sulu (pronounced sue-loo). I could give you all kinds of descriptions of it, its significance, etc, but here's the bottom line. My daddy didn't raise no fool. If it walks like a duck, looks like a duck, and quacks like a duck - it's not a chicken, it's a duck! Well, if it looks like a skirt, feels like a skirt, and you wear it like a skirt - you can call it a sulu, but it's really just a skirt! In this case, it was a colorful piece of fabric that you wrap around you to make a skirt over your shorts, and it was inscribed "Mona Island Resort." There were three blue ones and one pink one. Danno ended up with the pink one until he snatched mine out of my hands and said something lame like "I need yours, mine won't fit." At this point I figured, "I'm wearing a skirt in a primitive village on an island in the middle of nowhere, now is not the time to be worrying about how I look in pink!" I'm glad I didn't know it at the time but Danno was about to fall over laughing as we entered the chief's hut. The way I had tied my sulu had caused the words "Mona Island Resort" to be written across my posterior.

We sat down on bamboo mats and the four Fijian pastors, who had brought us in, began talking very loudly to the chief. We were trying to look nonchalant but I know we were all wondering what was going on. It seemed they were performing some kind of ceremony, and it was **loud**. I wondered if we were in some sort of demonic ceremony. After introductions, it was clear that the chief asked something like "So, what are the white boys doing here?" They explained and then we found out that he had a hurt wrist. To be honest, my rough and tumble buddies completely missed it, but I didn't. As uncomfortable in the natural as I was in these surroundings, I was suddenly in my element. Now, the chief is a Methodist and he hadn't experienced the renewal. He's not "church broke," i.e. he doesn't know how to assume the position of standing, eyes closed, with his hands out. He just stared at me as I laid my hands on his wrist and began to command any pain to leave. It did, very quickly.

THE CHIEF'S DEAF

Then he told his assistant to go get something, and he quickly came back with a new hearing aid. Now I understood – they were talking so loudly *because he's deaf.* Sometimes I wonder about my spiritual discernment. They told us there had been someone from the US who had come and tested his hearing and that's how he knew he needed a hearing aid. I was totally into this now. "God, do you want to do something here?" He did! We had already learned that you don't touch the chief's head without getting permission. The story goes that the first missionary to Fiji went to brush a bee off a chief's head and they killed and ate him (a long time ago they used to be cannibals). So, **don't touch the chief's head** is lesson #1 on a mission trip to Fiji! I got permission and sat crossed legged across from the chief and boldly stuck my fingers in his ears and commanded the spirit of deafness to go in the name of Jesus. I didn't even care that he was looking straight at me. I snapped my fingers by each ear in my best Benny Hinn impression and we learned that the hearing was back in the right ear. "Thank you, Lord." I prayed for the other ear a couple more minutes, tested it, and now he could hear perfectly out of both ears. We all talked in a normal tone for the rest of the ten minutes or so of our visit. And then it happened.

THE SILENT SOUND OF THE SPIRIT

When we left the chief's hut, I don't know how, but it was like the word was beginning to spread. It was like a sound - not audible, but a sound of the Spirit going forth - had gone out to the people of the village. I was aware that this was what it might have felt like when Jesus walked in Capernaum. There was a woman with a paralyzed baby waiting for us at the bottom of the steps to the chief's hut and we prayed for him. As we walked to the pastor's house, people were lined up for us to pray for.

I've often noticed that God honors those who serve. This was the case of the pastor who had driven the boat for us. He had problems breathing because his lungs had been damaged with all the diving he had done as a younger man; it's just part of their culture, being around the water so much. Bud and I prayed for him, out he went, and when he came-to he said he felt completely different and he could take deep breaths without pain, something he hadn't been able to do for quite some time. Then they took us to a woman's hut to pray for her legs and lungs. As Dave and I laid our hands on her feet and prayed for healing, I wondered about the hygiene of such an act. We were getting ready to eat lunch and there didn't seem to be any place to wash up. Lesson #2 on a mission trip is **always bring a small bottle of hand sanitizer.** Since I didn't have one I just prayed for the John G. Lake anointing, that all the germs would die and have no affect on us. It must have worked because none of us had any problems with the food.

A LONG, ROUGH BOAT RIDE

After the most incredible lunch of lobster you can imagine, they took us back to the shore to board our boat for the trip back to the main island where we would join the rest of the team. In many Asian cultures, you see young women holding hands as they walk down the street. This is a form of great affection for one another. In this culture, the grown men hold hands with those they like and admire. Danno obviously bonded with one of the Fijian pastors because they strolled to the boat hand in hand (I'll get you for giving me the pink sulu!).

As we hit the beach, we were in for a surprise, and a few more things began to come into focus. There were two boats full of about 15 white people getting ready to leave the beach area. They were from a nearby resort and they had come to pay homage to the chief so they could have lunch on the island where the movie "Cast Away" was filmed. It has turned into a tourist attraction. I can just see some Hollywood studio guy meeting with the resort people and the chief. "This is going to be a big movie, people are going to be willing to pay to go to that island, and we can all make money off this." I bet that's how an ear doctor was brought to test the chief's hearing and he got a hearing aid. I wonder if the Hollywood guy got fleas like we did; apparently the chief's hut has fleas, as Danno started itching immediately after he sat down and I noticed the bites on the plane ride home. He may be a chief, but the chief has fleas!

The next adventure was the boat ride back to the main island. We were going against the waves so there was a lot of pounding. It didn't help our confidence that a main runner below the driver's feet broke during this pounding. In typical macho fashion we all noted it and paid no attention to it outwardly. Later, however, we all confessed it was a matter of some concern to each one. The waves kept crashing over the back of the boat – right where Dave was. He got absolutely soaked for the next three and a half hours, as did Danno (Dave made sure of that). At one point, we ran out of gas and had to refuel from an extra tank. Each of us said later, but were afraid to admit it then, that we wondered what would happen if there was real trouble. They said there were three life vests and a flare gun on board, but we never saw them. Of course, there's a problem right there. I can do the math - there are six of us and three life vests? Some of us had already put in our dibs on pieces of the boat we hoped would float. There was no radio and no other boats on the water. How would we tell our wives what was going on and would we make it to the plane on time? Those are just some of the thoughts that go through your head at a time like that.

The final irony of the adventure was when Bud said they would be taking us to the marina to dock and we would walk to the hotel from there. The "marina" was the most rundown dock I'd ever seen, and when we finally got on the dock, Bud said "Make sure you step in the middle because sometimes the sides give way." I don't think I've ever been happier to be on dry land. After rejoining the team back at the hotel, hot showers, a clean change of clothes, a hearty meal, much kidding and telling the others what had happened that day, we finally made it to the airport, caught our plane, and arrived back on time in Vacaville. All of us said it was the most incredible adventure we had ever been on, and we got to see God's awesome power demonstrated in the most remote of places. For a moment I experienced what many missionaries go through who carry out God's work in remote, primitive places.

IF YOU WANT TO SEE MIRACLES, STEP OUT OF YOUR COMFORT ZONE

Carol and I have often wondered how our friends, Heidi and Rolland Baker, do what they do in such hard conditions in Mozambique. We've wondered if we could even do something like that for a week or two. The only thing I know is that I've said when you step out of the boat, out of your comfort zone, that's when you'll see miracles. While traveling with Randy Clark, I often heard him teach on the passage in Matthew 14 where it says Jesus "made" the disciples get into the boat and go to the other side. I believe, He knew He was sending them into to a storm because He wanted to develop character and obedience. In a way, that's what this felt like. I really didn't want to go on this boat out to the island, but I felt like there was something in this for me if I would just be obedient and go. Notice, in that same passage, that when Jesus came walking to them, they didn't recognize Him. This present move of God is much like that – God has come to us in ways that are new to us. This move doesn't look like the last move and too many people don't want to believe that it's God, or they don't want to believe He would, or could, come in such a way. But Peter became the brave one, asking Jesus if he could come to Him, and for a little bit he actually walked on water. You can't experience the full potential of God by only stepping out of the boat with one foot. You have to jump with both feet into the water. True faith is when you abandon yourself to it, when there's no turning back!

I can imagine Peter must have taken a lot of kidding from the rest of the disciples when he began to sink and had to cry out to Jesus, but look where he was – right in the arms of Jesus! Just think of the stories he was able to tell his grandkids: "Tell us about the time you walked on the water with Jesus, granddad." "Well kids, it was like this…" What a story he had, but it only happened because he was willing to risk, because he was willing to step out of the boat and out of his comfort zone in order to see the miracle. That's what happened for us on this adventure, an adventure I'm glad I didn't miss. And, maybe most importantly, I got a glimpse of what it must have been like when Jesus walked through Capernaum – people flocking to see and touch Him, and people getting healed. We were just co-laboring with Him and being His ambassadors - what an incredible privilege. That has been the journey through this renewal, the one that I'd like to tell you about.

CHAPTER 2

"THIS SICKNESS IS NOT UNTO DEATH"

"This sickness is not unto death." I took a lot away from the Healing Conference at Mott Auditorium in October 1995, but this phrase kept hitting me over and over when Evangelist Tim Storey said it, and it felt like it became a part of me. I remember thinking "How did I ever get into this place in my marriage?" You see, I knew this phrase was not about physical illness for me, but about the state of my marriage. Here I was with my marriage falling apart and I knew this was a prophetic word for me. Let me explain what was happening in my life at this point.

It would take too long to tell the whole story of how we got to this place (perhaps that's another book), but in the fall of 1995 Carol and I were in that hopeless, helpless place, heading toward divorce. I had been a successful Commercial Real Estate agent until God dramatically touched me on March 31, 1992 in Carol's Presbyterian church. She had become an ordained Presbyterian pastor, having graduated from Fuller Theological Seminary with a Masters of Divinity, and was an associate pastor of a Presbyterian church in San Diego. Carol was already filled with the Spirit when it happened to our daughter, Trish, and I. You would have thought life would have been wonderful from then on, but we've often said God had to do a work in us to get us to the place where He could then do the deep roto-rootering He needed to do with our marriage.

It had always been a marriage of form but no substance. We looked like the perfect couple. I was a businessman with all the prerequisite toys – large house with ocean view, high profile job, a

Mercedes and a Lexus, fancy ski vacations, investment properties and money in the bank. She was the perfect housewife who had become a pastor, and our daughter was in a private Christian school. But through a series of events it became obvious that God wanted to deal with our marriage and the baggage we had both brought into it twenty six years before. It became clear that we had both looked to others and to things for our identity, security, unconditional love and acceptance, worth, and purpose. Our needs were not being met through God, but in illegitimate ways.

By the fall of 1995 it had gotten so bad that everything we said or did hurt the other. We didn't mean to, but it was just too painful to be around each other. We had been in counseling for several months and we really liked our no-nonsense Christian counselor. I remember her saying she had great hope for us, even though we didn't. She also said that she didn't recommend separation because that was usually the first step to divorce. Still, on November 1st, about two weeks after this conference, that's exactly what we did. Carol moved out to a friend's house and I stayed in the condo we were renting.

SEPARATED - HEADED TOWARD DIVORCE

I had known the phrase Tim Storey said, "This sickness is not unto death," was referring to our marriage. I held on to that for a while, but it vanished in the hopelessness of the situation. On night shortly after Carol moved out, I even felt that I heard God say in my Spirit, "You can't even imagine what I'm getting ready to do. If you were to write a script, you wouldn't write it this way because it wouldn't be believable." I held onto these two prophetic words as long as I could, but in the pain and the hopelessness of our situation, it wasn't long before they slipped away.

Here was the situation as it existed at that time. Carol and some others had started a cell based church, which later became more of a missionary outreach to the poor in an area near downtown San

Diego. Several people they knew well had gone to some "Toronto" like meetings and came back with an attitude. They were basically saying "If you don't shake and bake, if you don't laugh and fall, you don't have what we have and you're missing God." This soured Carol and her group to the movement. I, meanwhile, was pursuing this move of God with everything I had and had begun attending the San Diego Vineyard, a church that was full blown into the renewal. My pastor, Gary, had counseled with both of us and was apprised of our situation.

Carol and I were separated for 6 weeks, and in the middle of that period we both came to the realization, independently and silently (until later when we compared notes), that we thought we knew where we were headed. We were both just trying to get through the holidays, to get into January and evaluate the marriage, and then begin the process of putting it to rest. But several things happened that were critical during this period. First, we stayed in counseling, even though the more we talked, the more hopeless it seemed. Second, when the counselor asked us to give a percentage figure of the degree of happiness we each had in the years of marriage, Carol saw that I didn't give up and run when her figure was only 20%. As you can see, this was not a great marriage. Third, the counselor had her ask me for something. This might not seem like a big deal, but Carol had always been someone who met everyone else's needs. She was a people pleaser, which meant she denied her own needs. It was a big step but the counselor actually had her express a need for me to meet, and I did. Fourth, she cut the ties to someone who was meeting her emotional needs on Friday, December 8th. It was never a physical relationship, but an "affair of the heart" and illegal just the same. This was a critical factor in our reconciliation because it broke something in the spiritual realm. Carol realized if there was any chance for our marriage to work, she needed to do this. But that didn't mean she was in a good mood when she arrived at the condo that afternoon to decorate the Christmas tree.

"MOM & DAD - YOU BELONG TOGETHER"

Our twenty three year old daughter Trish, with her hands clasped together, would say, "Mom and dad, you're mom and dad and you belong together." So it had been decided that we were going to decorate the tree like a family and then go to a play. Everyone was in their Christmas best, and I brought in the tree. The stand we had always used, however, didn't fit, as the tree trunk was too big. Since we had moved from our house to this condo I no longer had any tools, so I began frantically whittling down the tree trunk with a serrated kitchen knife. It didn't go easily, and soon I was sweating and ready to swear, and, you might remember, Carol wasn't in a good mood in the first place. The tension in the air was so thick you could almost cut it with that knife. Trish tried to fix the situation by exclaiming "Let's bake Christmas cookies, let's put on some Christmas carols - that will feel like Christmas." She was trying so hard to make it normal, but it wasn't to be. By the time we needed to go to the play, all we had succeeded in doing was getting the tree in the stand, but with no decorations. Trish said "We're not through so we have to come back on Sunday to decorate the tree," but Carol and I were both thinking "Oh, we are sooooo through!" The play that night – "Les Miserables." Very apropos don't you think?

CAROL COMES TO MY CHURCH

On Sunday afternoon, December the 10th, we gathered back at the condo. While we decorated the tree, to ease the tension in the air I told a story of what happened in my church that day. We had just moved into a new space in the shopping center the previous Sunday, and that night's renewal service was a real party. After about two and a half hours, a friend brought a young woman in her early twenties to me to pray for. She knew all this was of God, had experienced it all before, but had fallen away and was in sin, and couldn't "feel" anything. We prayed for her, she got gloriously touched and revived by the Spirit, and this Sunday morning had come running up to me and said it was the best week she had had in years. She was free and God had been present to her all week.

Carol remarked she had a friend who was living under a cloud like I had described on this young woman, and thought maybe she could bring her to church that night. Now, I have to admit my first thought was "Oh great, now she's going to invade my space, my only sanctuary from all this pain." But how do you tell someone they can't come to church, so I just smiled and said "That will be great." Carol and her friend arrived that night and we all sat together. The church was enjoying some great renewal services and this seemed to be like all the rest of them, but God was at work when I didn't even know it.

Now remember, Carol hated anything about the "renewal," but she actually enjoyed the worship, much to her surprise. Carol's heart was softening, and during worship she started thinking we ought to get prayer during ministry time. She asked me if I would with her to get prayer from the pastor, Gary. I didn't want to do this in the natural, but I heard myself saying "Sure." Since the worship team was playing during ministry time, we went back to a corner of the room so we could hear. Later, we found out they called this the "lost and found" corner for all the things left behind. God has a sense of humor - there was no one more lost and needing to be found than us.

Gary and a friend prayed for us, and I can't say it was anything earthshaking. Gary knew our general situation, but he prayed something that proved to be so prophetic. As he was praying for Carol, he said "Lord, let her find her identity in you." That was exactly what God had been talking to Carol about, that she was trying to get that need met through someone else rather than Him. When she closed the door on that relationship of the heart that Friday afternoon before coming to the condo, it opened the door for God to work in us that Sunday night.

Now, there have been times in this renewal when we both have experienced the electrifying touch of God, but this wasn't one of them. It was very gentle and we both "rested in the Spirit." When we both got up, Carol said it felt like she had been wearing smudged, cracked glasses that had been taken off, and she could see clearly. Our situation hadn't changed, but her perspective had. She asked me to go with her to take her friend home and on the drive back she said "We're supposed to be together, I need to move back in, and we need to get to Toronto as soon as possible." If you had told me this was going to happen an hour before I'd have said "no way" and I wouldn't have agreed to it, but I heard myself say "Ok." Something supernatural had happened in both our hearts and had softened them toward each other. When we met with our counselor that week, she was amazed, but she saw such a change in us that she thought it was totally God and she approved. Carol moved back in, and on Monday January 1st, 1996 we flew to Toronto to be there a week.

FROM SAN DIEGO TO TORONTO
IN JANUARY - CRAZY, DESPERATE

You have to be desperate for God to fly from San Diego, where it was 72 degrees, to Toronto in the dead of winter where it was 20 below without the wind chill factor. We knew we were in trouble when the hotel staff said the weather was "brutal" and the headline one day in the paper used the same word. But there we were and it was incredible. We had been told that even if the altar call is for blonde Swedish pregnant women, you go forward anyway for prayer. The church had just been disfellowshipped from the Vineyard on December 5th, it was the first week in January, and they were preparing for the second year anniversary celebration of the move of the Spirit on the 20th of the month, so there were only about 800-1000 people there. We got so much prayer – we became prayer hogs and it was all so good. God was doing such a deep work in our hearts toward each other.

On Friday nights they had a worship team that would leave the stage during ministry time and walk among the crowd playing. At one point Carol was prayed for by one of the faithful women of that prayer ministry team, and I caught for her. Since there wasn't a catcher for me, I just knelt on the floor for my turn. Carol said I was bathed in light from one of the overhead lights, and we ended up melted together in each other's arms. At that moment, the worship leader, his wife, and a violinist surrounded us and began playing "Arms of Love." We both thought we had gone to heaven. It was so beautiful, and our hearts were just further softened toward each other. We ended up staying up almost all night just talking, holding each other, and falling in love all over again. We recognized God had truly done a deep work in our hearts, and we decided we should write down our testimony in case they wanted to use it.

At one point Saturday afternoon Carol began talking about what we should do when we got back home on Monday. She wanted to go away, like on a second honeymoon, and process all that happened to us. I told her, "Well, we're in the honeymoon capital of the world right here." "We are?" she asked. "Yeah, Niagara Falls is only an hour away." I got hold of a travel agent, changed our flight home to the next Saturday, and made arrangements to go to Niagara Falls on Monday for three days. That night, they called out our names to come give testimony.

"RESTORE THE DREAM"

Now, up until Friday night all the prayer we had gotten had been very gentle and sweet, filled with the Love of the Father and anointed by the Spirit. But when Carol was standing on the line that night, a man on the ministry team came up to her, grabbed her hand, and said forcefully "Jesus, Jesus, Jesus!" It was actually quite loud and out of character with what we had previously experienced and Carol's first thought was "Nobody's going to push me over." In retrospect, I think he was just trying to hear the Lord because he got quiet and then said sweetly "Lord, restore the dream." We later learned that he is very anointed and hears clearly from the Lord.

Back in 1981, before Carol was even baptized in the Spirit, one of her charismatic friends told her of a vision she had had. In the vision she had seen Carol and me standing with our arms around each other's waist before a large crowd, and I was talking about Jesus. Carol had held onto that dream for a long time, and when I finally got saved, it seemed like it might even come true one day. In all of the pain in our marriage in 1995, however, she had forgotten the dream. When the prayer minister said, "Restore the dream," she said it felt like a hurricane had blown her off her feet. Could the dream really be true? Well, there we were, standing in front of a group of about 800+ people, arms around each other's waists, and I was talking about Jesus and what He had done in our marriage.

We have told people that from that moment on we are "puppy dog in love," and sometimes people who don't know our story will say "I always thought this was a second marriage for you two." And they're right – God didn't just heal a marriage, He created a brand new one. One of the incredible things is that He has used us to pray for other marriages and see them reconciled. We even got the chance to do that immediately, even though we broke the rules about praying for someone when you're not on the ministry team.

Somehow Carol Arnott had found out that our marriage had gotten healed there in Toronto and when we returned from Niagara Falls, she wanted us to go talk to a Danish couple. They were one of the foremost Christian marriage counselors in their country, but after 25 years their marriage was falling apart. I think Carol just wanted us to tell them what had happened for us, to give them some hope, but all of a sudden my Carol was praying for them. It didn't seem like anything happened and we walked away discouraged, but still thankful for the opportunity to pray for them. Then on the next to last day we were in Toronto, they happened to come walking into the cafeteria just beaming, arm in arm. They told us something had happened and they were falling in love all over again. Hey, God's in the business of restoring marriages!

NOT JUST A CHARGE - YOU NEED A NEW BATTERY

I said we originally went to Toronto for a week, but then extended to go to Niagara Falls for three days. Then, when we returned, several people on the prayer team began prophesying over us that God had more for us, and they encouraged us to stay for the second year celebration. Carol struggled with this at first. She didn't want to be someone who just chased after the "Holy Ghost goose bumps" like others she had seen. Then one afternoon, when the enemy was really attacking her during one of the intercession times, I prayed over her and she received a revelation from the Lord that silenced the lies of the enemy. She felt the Lord had said in her Spirit, "Sometimes, you get dry and, like a car, your battery needs to be recharged. Other times a recharging isn't enough – a new battery is needed and that takes a little longer. You need to stay because your battery is being changed and a new one is being put in." That made all the difference in the world for Carol, and we were able to extend our stay for another week and enjoy all God had for us in that three week period. We continued to be blessed by the teaching and the presence of the Holy Spirit, especially with all of the prayer ministry we got during this period, and we had one more encounter that was to leave quite an impression.

"NOT MORE - LESS, LESS"

On the next to last night, about 11:30pm, Carol and I both got prayer. We both went down in the Spirit, but I soon got back up. Fifteen minutes later, although aware of everything going on, Carol still couldn't get up. She was stuck to the floor! Her arms stuck straight out from her body like she was on the cross. That should have been the first clue. As I tried to bring each arm down to her side, it hurt her and it was like they were on springs because they would immediately "spring" back into the position of the cross when I let go. Since her arms were stuck out like that, I couldn't get her coat on, and it was still really cold outside. I also knew it would be very hard to maneuver in the shuttle bus with everyone else, so I knew I needed to do something because it was now almost midnight. I got her up, but she could barely walk and I had to support her from behind. Since we had been there for three weeks, many of the prayer team knew us by then. As some would walk by us, they would think it all looked funny and say "More, Lord, more." I was thinking that was one time they needed to pray "Less, Lord, less."

I figured I needed to get one of the prayer team members who had sort of taken us under her wing to help us, so I knew I needed to go find her. I was afraid to leave Carol "out" where the prayer team people might pray for her, so I stuck her in between two rows of chairs. But I could only stick her up to her arms, so her head was still sticking out into the aisle. It was truly a funny looking sight (Carol doesn't think so when I tell this part of the story). I found the prayer team member, and she was a lifesaver. She prayed for the anointing to lift off Carol and it did, partially. She was able to bend her arms at her elbow so we were finally able to get her coat around her. She drove us back to the hotel, and as soon as we got to the room, Carol had full use of her arms again. This manifestation served to teach us more about how the Holy Spirit works at times, and it helped us to be able to give explanations to others.

IT'S THE CROSS

Now, I didn't know what all that meant at the time, but Carol did and she didn't tell me. I thought we would be going home and I would be going to her church more and she would be coming to my church more – it would be more of a cross-pollination. Once again I had forgotten the word I had heard from the Lord. If I had written the "perfect" ending to all this, it would have been that she leave her church and come with me into the Vineyard and we would dive into the renewal together. But how could I ask her to give up her pastorate – something that was important to her, something she had gone to school for? But that's exactly what happened. God had been speaking to her about "going to the cross" to give up what she was holding onto but she didn't want to admit it, much less tell me. God had already told several of her friends in San Diego, however, and when we returned, they told her she would be leaving her church to join me. She suddenly "knew" God was speaking directly to her, and she was obedient. She resigned immediately, preached in that church one more time to say good-bye, and joined me at the Vineyard. We've been joined together in ministry ever since.

NEW MARRIAGE AND NEW MINISTRY

Our marriage was not only healed, but totally transformed. There's not a day that goes by that I don't thank God for what He did. And when we asked the Holy Spirit to come into our marriage, everything, and I mean **EVERYTHING**, changed for the better. We have known so many other marriages, many Christian marriages, that have gone through rocky times and haven't made it. Why ours? I think there were several factors: we stayed in counseling, we were totally submitted to wanting to be directed by the Spirit, Carol was obedient to break off the emotional tie she had that wasn't Godly, and we got ourselves into a place where the Spirit could work in our hearts so there would be true forgiveness. I also think that it was significant that at no time, even when it seemed so completely hopeless and I was discouraged, did I allow myself to think about what it would be like to be single again. I just didn't go there.

Finally, there's just something about the anointing in Toronto that is so conducive to healing. It's God's incredible mercy being poured out, and it hasn't stopped since 1994. In our travels now, we find people who are amazed that Toronto is still going on, five nights a week, all year long. And when we tell them that there are people coming from all over the world, many times 3000-5000 for one of the eight conferences a year they have, they are amazed. God hasn't stopped this renewal and it hasn't lessened - it has only grown bigger in many parts of the world. In the US, however, many have turned away believing the "river" has dried up or changed course, and they have moved on. In the next few chapters I want to give you a picture of the renewal from my vantage point. My prayer is that you'll see that the renewal isn't drying up at all, and that God wants all of us diving into His river.

CHAPTER 3

FULL ON RENEWAL BEFORE TORONTO

I got dramatically touched and transformed by God in a prayer meeting at Carol's Presbyterian church on March 31, 1992. Carol had become an ordained pastor, having graduated from Fuller Theological Seminary in 1988, and was an associate pastor at a Presbyterian church in San Diego. After my God encounter, we started having weekly Sunday night meetings at Carol's church. Everything that was to happen in Toronto in 1994 was happening then. We saw physical healings, prophesy, demons cast out, and people who would shake, cry, laugh and fall under the anointing of the Holy Spirit. I thought this was the norm for all Pentecostal/charismatic people, something I had missed out on in my main line denomination, and I actually wondered what all the fuss was about when Toronto hit. And from the moment I got touched, all I wanted to do was pray for people. Before that night, I had been in the church faithfully for 13 years, had no relationship with Jesus, heard very little about the Holy Spirit or satan, and I was trapped in demonically inspired sin. I had never prayed for anyone and no one had ever prayed for me – or at least I thought. I found out later that Carol and her gang of charismatic friends had me marked out on their prayer chain, and that there were times when Carol would wake up in the middle of the night and lay hands on me and pray, "God, get him." I didn't stand a chance – and I'm so grateful. That night of the prayer meeting, I got hooked on healing as I got to pray for Carol and she was healed.

MY LIFE IS TURNED UPSIDE DOWN

I had been a Commercial Real Estate Agent for 11 years, but suddenly it held no appeal for me. I began looking for opportunities to pray for people and God answered that desire. I went to prayer meetings, conferences, anything to be around the move of God. In 1994, I left the real estate business and began trading mutual funds for my own account on a computer program. That went well for a while, but after our marriage was transformed, it was like it was now time to deal with the spirit of mammon that had been operating in my life. It is said, "God loves you so much, He takes you just as you are and He loves you so much that He doesn't let you stay there." That's what was happening to me.

Carol and I were together in the Vineyard, we were being called upon to minister to people almost every day, but I can't say I trusted in my Heavenly Father yet. I would read the passage that says, "But seek first the Kingdom of God..." but my eye was always on my bank balance (Matthew 6:33). That's probably the main problem with our society today. We, especially men, are taught all our lives to depend on ourselves for our provision. I never heard the scripture that says, "For every beast of the forest is Mine, and the cattle on a thousand hills" (Psalm 50:10), or "The silver is mine, and the gold is mine,' says the Lord of hosts" (Haggai 2:8). I never heard, "...for it is He who gives you power to get wealth..." (Deuteronomy 8:18). Instead, all society told me, all that my earthly father ever told me, all that life around me told me, was to accumulate, to hoard for the rainy day. I never ascribed to "He who has the most toys when he dies wins," but I was close. Life was about having the big house, the prestigious car, money in the bank (and it could never be enough), and the investments for the future. It's the American dream that we all buy into. When I got touched at age 47 that stronghold didn't go away easily, and God had to deal with it. After all, I was praying this really dangerous prayer: "God I want to serve you; do whatever you have to do with me. God, have your way with me." You know, He takes our prayers way more seriously than we do.

INVESTING TO TRADING TO GAMBLING

I think deep in my heart I knew that the investing I was doing in the mutual funds had become trading and that, in 1996, the trading had become gambling. I think He may have been speaking to me about giving that all up, but I couldn't (or chose not to) listen. While I had a sizeable bankroll, it wasn't enough to live on without using it to make money. By the summer of 1996, I started losing large chunks of money. I can't begin to tell you how depressing that was. I was really seeking the Lord for answers, and at one point I thought He said to stop trading for two months. As soon as that was over, though, I started trading again because "I had to make money." The losses continued. Where before I had been very good at timing the market, now it seemed like I couldn't do anything right.

Finally, in November 1996, I stopped trading. Now we had no income coming in, but at least the money wasn't going out in large chunks. Still, every month, cha-ching, cha-ching - just like a cash register opening up, we would dip into our savings to pay the bills. Carol and I had gotten into a home-based multi-level business marketing nutritional supplements, and I wondered if that would be the vehicle that would allow us to make a living and minister too, but deep in my heart I didn't think so. Carol tried very hard to make it go, and there was a lot that she learned from doing the business that later applied to our ministry to come. I, however, was living under fear, and it was that fear that drove me back to my old work in November, 1996 - for a week. I realized then that I had absolutely no passion for the business - I felt like a fish out of water, and I just couldn't do it.

Three months later, in February 1997, I told myself that it was just fear talking, that I hadn't really given it a chance, and I went back to the same company to give it a real try. I've often said it shows how good a salesman I must have been to convince my old company to take me back twice. I don't know how sincere my effort was, but I only lasted two months this time. It was the same thing – there was no passion. It was a really embarrassing, humbling time for me. My co-workers didn't understand when I got born-again in 1992, and they *really* didn't understand when I came back into the business and then left abruptly, twice. But I just knew I wasn't supposed to be doing this, knew that I was supposed to be giving myself to the ministry. Part of the confusion was I had never felt called to go to seminary or bible college, so I couldn't see how this would ever lead anywhere. How could you exist just praying for people? All I knew was I just wanted to pray for the sick, teach about this present move of God, and flow wherever the renewal took me. Even so, after I left the real estate business again, an incredible opportunity for ministry came up.

SHE DIDN'T KNOW HOW TO
CONTEND FOR HER HEALING

I went to pray for a friend in the hospital who was having gall bladder surgery. The woman in the next bed heard us praying and asked if I and my prayer partner would come back and pray for her, as she had just been diagnosed with terminal cancer. We had the incredible privilege of praying for this 29 year old nominal Christian and speaking into her life about the fullness of God, and the power of the Holy Spirit.

One of the things Carol and I learned from Randy Clark was to never just to tell our success stories, because some people will compare themselves to you and say they could never do what you do. They often don't hear about the times when you pray for someone and they don't get healed. This story has both. We got to pray for this woman three times in the hospital, and three more times at home. After the second time of prayer she had her first chemo treatment. They told her they had never seen the chemo work like that but the cancer was gone, and they were talking cure! They couldn't recognize the power of prayer but we knew what was happening to her.

I wish I could say there was a happy ending to this miracle, but over the course of the next few months she quit getting prayer and we lost track of her. Five months later she called back to say the cancer had returned in full force. Carol and I prayed for her several times and got her to some renewal meetings, but she died of this cancer. This was one of those times when I didn't have the answer. I think she wasn't strong enough in the Lord and didn't know to fight when the enemy tried to come back. One of the things we've seen in our ministry is that often the enemy will come back in and try to steal your healing. After all, just because we're Christians, we don't have a hands off policy from the enemy. You have to fight against the enemy when he comes back. We often quote that scripture that says, "Therefore submit to God. Resist the devil and he will flee from you." (James 4:7). You have to fight against the enemy when he comes back.

In one of our Saturday afternoon meetings we prayed for a man with chronic back pain that he had been dealing with for 12 years. All the pain left, but we told him and the rest of the church to guard against the enemy coming back in to steal the healing, that you need to stand and say "No!" When we saw him at church the next day, sure enough he had awakened with pain again. He remembered what we had said, though, and rebuked the devil, commanding the pain to leave - and it did! I think that's what happened with this woman. She didn't know enough to do these things, because it was all so new to her and we were only given a little access into her life. Still, we were grateful to be a part of her life and to have the privilege of praying for her, and it wouldn't have happened if I had been working full time.

BEING STRIPPED

For the rest of 1997 and half of 1998 we lived on our savings, which were going down at a rapid rate. I've really struggled with this over the years and still don't know that I have a good explanation for the wisdom of this. Was God in this? I think God probably had several ways I could have gone, but in my state of mind about money, I could only go down this road, and it was the most painful one. One of the things I learned about God during this process was He isn't co-dependent like most of us are.

After I was saved I was shocked that everything wasn't suddenly going perfectly. When I was going through this trial I kept expecting Him to come riding up on a white horse and rescue me. After all, as parents we have done the same many times for our daughter, because we can't stand to see her get hurt. God knows what's best for us, however, and rescuing us isn't the best way. I think I had to go through this, and as painful as it has been, I have come to rely more on the goodness of my Father, and know He is always there for me. It's a process and it is ongoing. He is my provision, and now I'm starting to understand that I work for Him and if I will seek first the Kingdom, He will take care of me. I don't think that if I seek the Kingdom my worries will all be taken care of, but if I will seek first the Kingdom, I'll find that the Kingdom comes fully equipped. This period of stripping also taught me that I was finally passionate for something and, like the song goes, "I'm desperate for You." All I wanted to do was pray for people and be near the move of God. I continued to go to as many conferences as I could, and to pray for as many people as I could. By this time we had been made Pastors of Prayer at the Vineyard church we went to and we were doing a lot of training in prayer ministry.

"YOU'RE CURSED WITH A CURSE"

In March 1998, we had an event happen that revolutionized our ministry and the way we looked at money. Rodney Howard Browne came to town for five days of meetings. At that time, he felt he had a mandate from God not only to bring the power of the Spirit in his meetings, but to also teach on giving. He would teach for 30-45 minutes on giving, and then he would preach for an hour before beginning ministry. It was revolutionary teaching for us. We thought it was like manna from heaven, but it was amazing how many people got offended and wouldn't come back to the meetings.

Now, prior to these meetings, Carol had gotten the verse Malachi 3:9. She didn't remember what it said, but when she looked it up she saw, "You are cursed with a curse." She knew it was about tithing, but she didn't think it could apply to us. Even though we had almost no income coming in, we were very generous each week and were giving faithfully to the church and to others when there were needs. She got the verse again after the meetings with Rodney, however, and started asking the Lord what this was about.

He said we were cursed with a curse because we had withheld a pledge. When Carol told me about what she had heard, I felt like I had been hit with a ton of bricks. It all started to fall into place.

In May of 1996 we had gone to a missions conference at Harvest Rock church in Pasadena. Pastor Che Ahn had challenged all of us to ask the Lord what He would have us give, and if we didn't have it at the time, to pledge to give it when the Lord provided it. Carol and I each heard the exact same figure, independently of each other - $10,000. We both knew this was God because we had never even considered anything near this kind of figure before. I easily had this amount in 1996, but my mindset was that I had to have money to be able to trade the mutual funds, so I pledged to give the amount when the Lord provided it. I had the money, but I withheld it from the Lord. Bad move.

As this realization came to me, I began furiously paging through my day planner from 1996. Sure enough, that conference was May and I began losing large chunks of money in June. I knew there was a direct correlation. Furthermore, I knew I needed to make good on that pledge. I knew that I knew that I knew this was God and even though that check in March 1998 represented 1/3 of all the money we had, I immediately wrote that check and sent it off to the church. As fearful as I was about being in this place and seeing the bank account dissolve, I never hesitated a moment about writing that check. It was God's grace on me, and I had a peace about it because I knew we had to do it.

"IF YOU WANT REVIVAL, SOW INTO REVIVAL"

We also took to heart something else Rodney said during that week: he said if you want to see and sow into revival, you can do that by giving into a ministry that produces good fruit for revival. We decided to begin sowing monthly into two ministries that I thought were producing good fruit – Rodney's ministry and Randy Clark's. Now, I had never met Randy but I had been to several meetings he had done. I liked his laidback style, and I particularly liked the healing anointing he walked in. I read all the reports of his meetings that were posted on the internet, and I knew he sometimes took people on foreign mission trips with him. I had such a strong desire to go to Argentina, because of the revival going on down there and, in the winter of 1998, I applied to be on a team going in May for which I was accepted.

I had also been asked by my pastor, Gary, to go with him on a missions trip to Korea. I was in hog heaven. We would go to Korea for 10 days in May, be home for a week, and then I would go on a 14 day trip with 15 people to Buenos Aires and Cordoba, Argentina. The trip to Korea was paid for, but I would have to pay for the Argentina trip.

In early May, the team got notification that there had been severe flooding in Argentina and they were going to have to reschedule the trip. I was very disappointed, but that still left the trip to Korea. It was an incredible trip. We saw a lot of healing, and I saw a lot of power when I ministered.

While we were in Korea, Randy Clark went to California to do meetings at Bethel Church in Redding, Family Christian Center in Orangevale, and Vaca Valley Christian Life Center in Vacaville. On the first night in Redding, there were 138 people healed as Randy gave words of knowledge for healing. He had been used to seeing this kind of results in foreign countries, but not here in the US - usually, the most he would see healed in the US was about 30. In reading the reports I knew something was happening. There was a healing anointing that was being released in Northern California that we weren't seeing in Southern California, and I wanted it. In the subsequent reports it was determined that since he wasn't able to go to Argentina, he would come back to California and spend a week at Vacaville in the latter part of June – I knew I had to be there.

CHAPTER 4

I MEET RANDY CLARK

Now, I know it makes no sense that I had just been off ministering in Korea, had no job or income, and very little savings left. Believe me, I've wrestled with this dilemma many times. It has caused fits to my little left-brained, logical mind. It made no sense, but it was like I couldn't do otherwise. I even went to two days of training with a residential real estate company when I returned from Korea, but I just couldn't commit to working there full time. All I know is if I had looked at everything from only a logical position, I would have gone back to work then. And if I had, I certainly couldn't have gone to the meetings in Vacaville. I just knew I had to go to those meetings in Vacaville at the end of June 1998, though. I didn't see it at first, but it was like I had special favor, and God's grace all over me.

I GOT ON THE MINISTRY
TEAM FOR THE CONFERENCE

I had talked with both Randy's office back in Saint Louis and with the Vacaville church about being available to help on the prayer team for the conference, and they said I could. I was going for two reasons: I figured if I could sit under Randy's teaching and be on the ministry team under his anointing, maybe something would rub off. And since the trip to Argentina was canceled, I wanted to know if he might be taking a team with him on his upcoming trip to Australia in September. Once again, I *know* this makes no sense, because by the end of June we had figured we had enough money to last us to the end of August if nothing changed in our financial picture. But off I went on Monday morning to arrive in time for the first meeting that night.

I had planned to go only through Friday, but on the eight hour drive up from San Diego I felt like I heard the Lord say "don't be in a hurry to leave." I arrived in time to check into the Motel 6 near the church and prepare for the night meeting. I have to admit, this trip was starting off on a humbling note. I had been used to staying in nicer motels in the past, but with my financial picture being what it was, I couldn't justify staying at anything costly. Surely God must have noticed my desperation.

A DIFFICULT CHOICE?

When I walked in, I was amazed. It was a big Assembly of God church with a sanctuary that would hold about 800. I met several of the pastors, and the man in charge of the ministry team, Mark, made me feel at home. The meeting turned out to be everything I had hoped for and we finished up about 11:30 PM. I was just about to walk out the door to go back to the motel when a defining event happened that the pastor, Randy, and I still joke about.

Mark told me Randy and several people were going over to pastor Dave's house for snacks and asked me if I wanted to come. Hmmmm - go back to a lonely Motel 6 room, or go hang out with Randy Clark and the pastors. Tough decision — but I said, "Sure." There was no logical reason to include me, but I think that he somehow thought I was connected in some way with Randy's ministry, Global Awakening. I later found out that everyone else was wondering who I was. At one point Dave went up to Randy and asked him, "Who's this guy, Bill Dew, with you?" Randy said, "I don't know him, I thought he was one of yours." The Vaca Valley people thought I was with Randy, and Randy thought I was with them. But there I was, sitting around the table with Randy and the pastors, talking about the move of God and telling Holy Ghost stories until 3 AM. We did that every night that week - I thought I was in hog heaven! It was then that I began to understand Randy's crazy schedule, because we would have to get up for 10 AM meetings the next day.

I BECOME RANDY'S DRIVER

That next night, I happened to see Dave at about 6:15 and asked him if Randy was there yet. I still don't know why I asked him that - it was once again God's favor on me. Dave looked startled as he suddenly realized they hadn't sent anyone to pick up Randy and Ben, the 18 year old young man he was mentoring. I said I would go get them if he wanted. After the meeting they asked me if I would drive Randy and Ben back to the hotel, and then Dave sheepishly asked about the Thursday afternoon meeting.

They had scheduled Randy to do a meeting at a church in Napa, about an hour away. Since I was there with nothing else to do but be there for the meetings, Dave asked me if I would mind driving Randy and Ben over there and back. Now, I was excitedly think-ing, "I'll have to take him to lunch, drive an hour in the car with him, do the meeting with him, drive him back and have dinner with him." I tried to act cool as I said, "Yeah, I guess I could do that." I had just been hoping to get near him so maybe something would rub off – now I was going to have him in my car, picking his brain, ministering with him. I figured something's bound to rub off! And this is honestly true - there were several times when I leaned over to get something from the glove box. Not because I needed anything, but because it gave me an excuse to "accidently" rub up against him. Yes, I was that desperate. I had a great time being with him, but I think he picked my brain just as much as I picked his. He had learned I had been a commercial real estate agent, and he was trying to sell his church building back in Saint Louis. He had lots of ques-tions and I tried to help him as much as I could.

DEBORAH'S PROPHETIC
MINISTRY GIVES ENCOURAGEMENT

I went to every day and evening meeting that week and extended my stay through the last meeting Sunday night. Carol was at home, but a friend needed to come to Northern California, and they decided to come to Vacaville before the friend would move on. It was unusual for Carol to do that, to drive up 8 hours on a Saturday to turn around again and drive back another 8 hours on Monday. Something was up for both of us.

The pastors on staff and many of the ministry team knew she was coming and were looking forward to meeting her. On Saturday night, Randy gave his message on "God Can Use 'Lil Ole Me." You might ask, "How can you remember that?" I can't but I have the notes from those meetings. I've never been a big note taker, but all during that week I took notes on what was said, the words of knowledge given, and how many were saved and healed. I didn't know it at the time, but I was in training for my assignment when I would travel with Randy - I would need to take copious notes because I would write the reports on virtually every meeting for 16 months.

That night, God was all over Carol. She was shaking and crying under the power of the Holy Spirit and we both went forward during the ministry call. After Randy prayed for us, Dave's wife, Deborah, prayed for us. She's very prophetic and basically read our mail, and gave us some much needed encouragement. She said, "You have made a deposit into the Kingdom and now God is making a deposit in you." She didn't have a clue about our financial condition, but remember - we had just recently written that $10,000 check to fulfill the pledge we had made back in 1996. Then she, and later her prayer partner, Tammy, saw independently of each other that we were like rockets or arrows being shot out, and that God would give us the weapons we would need.

WE GET LAUNCHED - SHOT LIKE AN ARROW

Deborah also saw a picture of Carol in a bright yellow sundress, ministering to the Lord. How could she have known that one year later we would all be on a team together in Brazil with Randy, and Carol would wear a bright yellow sundress, having completely forgotten about this prophesy? But Deborah didn't forget and reminded us. We were able to check it against our notes from that night, and we weren't through with that arrow thing being launched.

After midnight on Saturday, after almost everyone had left, Mark and Tammy and another couple who had bonded with us, Dave and Devi, felt like they were to pray over us and symbolically launch us. The floor of the sanctuary could also double as a basketball court, and had a circle in the middle. They felt like they were to have us lie face down side by side in the circle, place an arrow on each of our backs, and pray for God to launch us out into the ministry He had for us. I don't know what they thought they were doing but I know what we thought - it was symbolic of our being launched into a greater anointing for healing, deliverance and prophesy and we would be bringing it to our church, and maybe even affecting our city of San Diego. In hindsight, we can now see it was about a greater launching than we could ever have imagined.

THEY NEEDED A KEEPER

One of the things Randy is famous for is being an idea man, a right brained individual whose mind is racing way ahead of the everyday things. He recognizes this and knows he can't be trusted to be given anything important - like money - because he'll lose it immediately. He needs someone with administrative abilities to handle the details, and that had been one of the functions of Bill Cassada. Bill and his wife, Barbara, had traveled and worked with Randy for a year but had left a month before to become one of the Global Awakening Resource Teams, teaching and ministering as Randy did. Now Randy had an extraordinarily gifted young man of

18 traveling with him named Ben. He was mentoring him, but the problem was that he was exactly like Randy, and they both needed a keeper.

When Carol and I drove Randy back to the hotel on Sunday night after the closing party at Pastor Dave's house, Randy said something funny as he started to walk into the hotel. It was as if the Lord was speaking to him. He turned and asked, "Are you very organized? I may need some help." Carol immediately jumped in and started listing my ability to handle details in real estate; the faithful wife looking out for her husband. Then he told me to write to his secretary, because he would forget, and tell her that we had talked about my desire to go to Australia. Then he went inside and that was it.

On the drive home the next day we kept asking ourselves what happened the night before: "Was he thinking of me traveling with him? But he hadn't asked me. It seemed like he was almost listening to God talk to him, though. Do you think anything could come of this – no. And how would I do it anyway with our financial condition? But what if he wanted me to travel with him some..." As you can see, we went back and forth in great excitement, but not really knowing what he meant the night before. I so wanted to think something like that could happen, but I was afraid to get my hopes up. I wrote a letter to his office, told him I would love to go with him to Australia if he decided to take anyone, and if I could help in any way, I would make myself available. After a few weeks passed and I had heard nothing, my hope dissolved and I figured nothing would come of it.

RANDY CLARK CALLED "LITTLE OLE ME"

Then on a Friday night, exactly a month from that week in Vacaville, we returned home from a conference at midnight. I checked the answering machine and literally almost fell off the chair. In Randy's typical, homey Southern accent he drawled, "Hi Bill, this is Randy. I wanted to ask you if you'd like to travel with me for a year. I need some help with the book table and other administrative things, and you'd also be in the meetings helping me minister." He finished by saying he was going to Africa on Monday, so try to call if I could before then. It was midnight in San Diego, so it was 2 AM in St. Louis.

Now, I am usually pretty stable emotionally - not too high or too low, but I have to admit that I got excited, like a kid in a candy shop. I looked at Carol and said "Randy Clark called 'lil ole me. Randy Clark! Do you think it's too late to call him? Oh yeah, of course it is. I don't want to sound too anxious. But if I wait I might miss him? He might rethink his offer - he might not want me to travel with him. How are we going to pay for this? Oh yeah, where there's a mission, there's provision." These were the things that were going through my head and out of my mouth, and I was talking a mile a minute. We were both excited. I finally decided that I'd better wait until about 9 the next morning to call, which would be 11 his time. I didn't want to seem too anxious, but I wanted to time it so he'd be there and not out doing afternoon errands.

Needless to say, sleep didn't come easy that night. All I had wanted to do was travel and minister, to pray for people, especially for healing. I never saw how or believed that it could happen, but Carol tried so hard to get me centered on looking to God for the answers. Something about Seek *first* the Kingdom, and all these things would be added unto you. And here was Randy, giving me the chance to do exactly what my heart had been crying out to do.

When I finally talked to Randy the next day, he outlined what he wanted to see happen and how I could help him. He needed someone to help with the book table that was set up at each meeting, and to help with the general administrative details while on the road. Of course, the thing I was looking at the most was the fact that I would also be helping him with ministry. When we finished discussing all of these things he made me the offer: "I can't pay you anything and you have to pay your own way." I would be able to stay with him in the hotel room most of the time, so that would hold down the cost some. I've often joked that I was in real estate and I knew what a good offer was – this was not a good offer for someone in my position. But Carol and I prayed about it and we felt like we heard two things. We felt like God was saying I was to trust Him completely and to go with Randy. I also felt like I heard that I was to be a servant for a year, and to lay down any agenda I might have. I knew this would be a challenge - after all, I was pretty much a type A kind of guy and was used to speaking and leading. Now I would be a servant. I decided to answer the call, but I still had to find a way to pay for it.

CHAPTER 5

GOD HAD ALREADY RAISED MONEY
FOR THE FIRST TWO TRIPS

When I thought I was going to Argentina, I had raised $2400 towards the trip, as suggested by Randy's office. I got permission from those contributors to use this money to travel with Randy now instead. I began sending out letters asking for support, mostly to our Pentecostal/charismatic friends, but also to my real estate and tennis buddies, most of whom weren't saved. Interestingly, the first contribution I got was on the tennis court from my weekly partner. He said, "Bill, you know I don't believe in God, but I believe in you." I've prayed often over every one who has contributed into our ministry, that they would get a realization that they have partnered with us, as it talks about in Philippians 4:15-16. And I pray that the "fruit that abounds" would abound to their account (Philippians 4:17).

Another key help at this time was our friends Michael and Georgette. They offered to host a party for us where we could share our vision of what God was doing with us in my traveling with Randy and funds could also be raised. They have been very supportive of us throughout this whole process, and we are forever indebted to them.

A month after Randy's phone call, I took off on August 24, 1998, to join him and Ben for meetings in Florence, Kentucky, after which we would fly to England for more meetings. I arrived at the church at the end of the afternoon meeting, met Cleddie Keith, the pastor, and waited for Randy to come for the evening meeting. You know how it is to start a new job - you feel uncomfortable and unsure, wondering if you really fit in, etc. That's what it felt like waiting. When Randy came in, however, he was very gracious and made me feel right at home. At the end of the meeting, when we were all gathered back in the lounge and they were discussing where we were staying, he grabbed me and said to the hosts, "Can he please stay with us?" I'm sure it had all been arranged beforehand but it was a defining moment for making me feel at home and immediately a part of the team.

"EYE, BE STRAIGHT." IT WORKS!

The meetings at Cleddie's church went really well, and I immediately saw the fruit of sitting under Randy's anointing and the incredible atmosphere at Heritage Fellowship. That Sunday afternoon was our last meeting, and we did a healing service. At one point I went to check on the book table, and when I walked back into the room, almost everyone had been prayed for and many were still on the ground. I asked the Lord if He wanted me to pray for anyone. I felt he directed me to a beautiful 12-year-old girl lying on the floor. She told me she had pain in her ankle, and that she also had a wandering eye that couldn't focus.

Now, to be honest, I didn't have a lot of faith for that eye, but I'd already heard Randy teach on not turning that principle of faith into a law. If you turn it into a law, then what do you do when there's a need in front of you but you don't have enough faith? This is why we teach and quote Nike's slogan, "Just do it!"

I went for the foot. Pretty soon it got hot and she began moving it all around with no pain. I started to realize that those things Randy was teaching were true, so I went for the eye next. I had already heard Randy tell the story the time the Vineyard team came to his little Baptist church in Spillertown, Illinois. One of Randy's friends in the church, John, got a word of knowledge for the eyes, which led to them praying for a 14 year old girl who had crossed eyes along with other complications. One of them had placed his hand on her eyes and said simply, "In the name of Jesus, eyes be straight." It took 5 times but they were suddenly straight. Now, to be honest, I thought that if Randy and his friend had to pray 5 times, it would probably take me 10 times. I figured that girl was 14, this girl is 12, let's not reinvent the wheel here. So I just placed my hand over her eyes and said, "Eyes be straight, in the name of Jesus" (I didn't want to just totally copy him). I took my hand off her eyes and asked her how it was. It looked different to me, like it was straight. I began having her follow my finger up and down and all around. I don't know who got more excited, her or me. We did this for what seemed like 10 minutes and the eye was tracking perfectly with the other, something she said had never happened. I walked out of that meeting like I was walking on air. This is what I had been longing to see and experience. The next day, Randy, Ben and I, Cleddie, and Scott, a businessman Cleddie often brought on trips with him, took off for London.

I TOOK OVER THE REPORTS

The meetings were to be with Wes Richards' church in Slough, outside of London. The next 5 days were to be a time of getting to know Ben, and also seeing where we were in the pecking order. Randy, Cleddie, and Scott stayed at a very nice home, where we would go after the meetings to dine and wind down. Ben and I went to the church's home for unwed mothers. There were many rooms that would house these women, and they kept one room off to the end for guests. It was sparse, but comfortable. The good thing was it was in Windsor, so we could walk into town and play tourist with the rest of the crowds coming to see the Windsor Castle. This actually worked out well as Randy needed to fly home on Saturday, but Ben wasn't flying out until Sunday with me. We did a bunch of shopping for his girlfriend and my family, and we got to know each other some. He's an incredible young man, very gifted, and as we traveled together for the next 16 months he continued to grow in his gifting, especially for deliverance. It was during this time that I began taking over the report writing from him.

Randy had had most of his meetings recorded – I especially remember reading reports from Rick Stivers and Bill Cassada. These reports were always inspiring as they told what God was doing around the world, and I know many people were encouraged by them. I often read from or quoted these reports to inspire our prayer team during our pre-service meetings. It was important to me to see this continue and it was something I wanted to do. But at that point I was not very knowledgeable with a computer and I know I drove Ben and Randy crazy because I just couldn't seem to get the hang of what they were trying to tell me about how to work the laptop. I did persevere, however, and then the only problem I had was getting time on either Randy or Ben's computer. They took note of this and Rex, who traveled with Randy the following year, was given his own computer.

Randy's last night of meetings was to be at a large gathering called Grapevine. We rented cars to drive up there and thankfully Scott, who had driven in England before, was our driver instead of me. I think they noticed how nervous I was about driving on the other side of the road. That didn't mean I got out of it, however. When we came back to London, we dropped Randy and Scott off at the airport, and now I had to drive the car back to turn it in to the rental place. The car had a left-handed stick shift, we were driving on the left-hand side of the road, and we had to get through the congested traffic leaving Gatwick Airport. We went around several round-a-bouts a couple of times because I just couldn't get into the right lane to leave. It's funny to think about now, but it wasn't then.

I GET TO AUSTRALIA — AND NEW ZEALAND

We came home for about a week, and then came the trip I had been waiting for – we were going to Australia and New Zealand. I met Randy and Ben in Los Angeles, and we flew into Sydney at night. We were staying at a beautiful hotel, and I knew this was going to be one of the first big tests. With my limited finances, I really didn't need to be paying for a room myself, but the Australian team had seemed reluctant to want to put us all into one room. The room was perfect, however, with a separate bedroom and a fold out couch for me.

The next morning we were able to see what we had missed by coming in at night - the hotel faced Botany Bay and had the most gorgeous view. We met the pastor of the church, Frank Houston, for lunch, and he took us to a restaurant at a mall. I had known I was going to be meeting many apostolic men and women while traveling with Randy, but now it was happening. I didn't realize it until then, but this 76 year "young" man was the superintendent of the Assemblies of God in Australia, and his church had birthed many churches around the world, one of which was pastored by his son, Brian. Several years before, Brian had taken about 45 people from this church and planted a new church in an affluent area of Sydney called "Hills." They were particularly known for their worship, which they called "Hillsong." I had been lamenting that their worship team was going to be in San Diego while we were in Australia, and here I was where it had all been birthed.

"WE HAVEN'T TRAINED THEM IN DELIVERANCE, HAVE WE?"

We would be doing a "Catch the Fire" conference with Ken Gott. I was excited because I had heard of him, but had never been to any of his meetings. As with Randy, I found him to be very down to earth, very humble, and with a great sense of humor. Several interesting things happened in this conference.

As Randy was speaking one evening, I could tell he was going down the road to deliverance. This ministry had become very important to Randy, especially after meeting with Carlos Annacondia in Argentina. Since then, Randy had been bringing Pablo Botarri, who had been Carlos's deliverance minister for 11 years, to the US to teach on deliverance. Whenever Randy had prayer ministry training done, this deliverance training was a major part of it. I leaned over to Ben and asked, "Have they had the deliverance training?" He said didn't think so. It wasn't a minute later that Randy looked over at us and said "Oh, oh, I've put the cart before the horse. We haven't taught them on deliverance have we?" He was too far down this road to turn back, however, so he went for it.

There were about 900 in the conference and when Randy gave the call for those who struggled with habitual sin, it seemed like three fourths of them came forward. When he began coming against the spirits that had been holding them in bondage, there were all sorts of manifestations. Many had to be carried off to a room they had designated for deliverance. I quickly sent a sheet I had on the Ten Step Deliverance Model to be Xeroxed by one of the church secretaries.

I entered the deliverance room where my worst fears were realized. There were people all over the floor, rolling and screaming. Many were being held down while several in each group were screaming at the top of their lungs for the evil spirits to come out. There were at least 100 people to receive ministry. I quickly began going to each group, handing out the sheet, telling them if they would just tell the spirit to submit in the name of Jesus and then read the directions off the sheet, it would go much easier. I got a lot of looks like, "Yeah right, mate," but when I left the room about 5 minutes later to go get more sheets, I realized it had gotten quiet. They were actually reading off the sheet and following the directions. We've often told the groups that we train in deliverance not to be worried about this ministry, that they are getting much more training than the Australians, and they handled it beautifully!

RANDY AND HIS TWO DEMON CHASERS

The next night, Ken Gott got Randy. He started going down a road that would lead to taking up the mantle of your ministry, like Elisha had gotten from Elijah, and we were getting excited because we wanted prayer from Ken. Then he said, "But you can't take that mantle until you've dealt with the sin that's kept you in bondage. So, Randy and his two demon chasers, Ben and Bill, are going to minister deliverance to you and then when you get free come back in here."

Now you need to know, Randy is great at stirring the demons up. He got the Annacondia anointing when he met him. But he hates *doing* deliverance. When you travel with Randy, one of the worst things you can hear is Randy calling over the microphone "Oh Bill, could you come over here, I need you." What's happened is, he's stirred up some demons, but he doesn't want to deal with them, so he calls you. Or someone taps you on the shoulder and says, "Randy sent me" and you can tell from their eyes it's not about blessing.

We were in that room until about 2 AM, both Ben and I, at different times, dealing with the "bride of satan." She had been dedicated as a child and suffered terribly. We got a certain degree of freedom for her, but it wasn't complete. When we finally caught up to Ken back in the hospitality lounge, the meeting was long over and he was too tired to pray for us. He left the next day, and I've not run into him since. Ken Gott, you owe me a prayer.

I was so wrapped up in this trip that I barely noticed that the only thing we did was go from the hotel to the church and back. Aside from that one trip on the first day to a restaurant in a mall, we hadn't seen anything. Actually I had been conditioned for this. At times I had traveled with Mark McCoy, the worship leader for the San Diego Vineyard, and we had taken the position that we would "gladly spend and be spent" for the gospel (2 Cor.12:15). But after the conference Randy was to minister at a sister church in a suburb about an hour away. As we drove over a bridge near downtown, I recognized the tips of the Sydney Opera House sticking up. That become the lone tourist stop I could say that we saw on our trip to Australia.

THE HONEST CONFESSION

The next day we flew to New Zealand where we were picked up by Craig, who had arranged for Randy to come to his country. It was the hungry, desperate cry of a man who wanted to see revival for his country and for his town of Palmerston North. He wasn't even the pastor, but Randy's office didn't realize this. We had some great meetings there, but I was to learn something startling there, and Randy was to receive some books that would speak into his ministry and as have a profound effect on all of the Global Awakening Associates.

In a meeting one night I heard Randy say "Did you know you can be dry in the middle of the river?"

Wait a minute, are you saying that you're dry? You? Mr. Toronto - the one responsible for starting this river in Toronto that has gone around the world? That's what I was thinking as I heard those words come out of Randy's mouth. But what he was saying was that in the midst of traveling and doing meetings around the world, as wonderful as it all was, he had gotten dry.

It was a wakeup call. His schedule had gotten hectic in the months before I had joined him, and the schedule coming up didn't look easy either. And Randy was tired. His honesty came flowing out; I think that's what has endeared him to so many people around the world. What you see is what you get. He is very honest, self revealing and transparent. But Craig gave him two books that spoke to the hunger in him, and ultimately to all of us associated with him. It was a set of two books called "William Branham: Supernatural." They traced the early years of this very controversial and anointed healing evangelist, until about 1950. Since then, the author has released three more books, and is doing the research on the last book, which will document the rest of Branham's life. Those books so inspired and lit a fire in Randy that he got a set for each of the associates who came to the planning meetings the next month. It was literally that one thing that touched the place of hunger for the things of God in him, and it rekindled his passion again. It wouldn't be the last time that he would need a jump start.

GOD BLESSES THE SERVANT HEART

I saw another thing happen, one that I was to see repeated many times over. God loves to bless and honor the hungry servant. Craig had been very desperate and hungry for renewal to come to New Zealand, and he had worked tirelessly to set up these meetings and get Randy there. And he had a health problem - passing a kidney stone is as close as we men can get to childbirth, and Craig had had constant pain and problems with them for over two years. After the first night's meeting was done, I walked up to him and put my finger on his heart and began praying for him. He told me then, and has told me since, that it felt like electricity was coursing through his body, unlike anything he has ever felt. I didn't realize it at the time, but there's actually scriptural reference for this. In Habakkuk 3:4, it says "His brightness was like the light; He had rays flashing from His hand, and there His power was hidden. " I've since actually experienced that and have prayed for others to get it, and many have. At one point in Brazil, there was actually electricity coming from my hands, and almost everyone I prayed for felt like they had been "electrocuted."

About the same time I started praying for Craig, Randy put his hands on his kidneys. Craig vibrated for the next 45 minutes, sweating profusely and turning bright red despite his fair complexion. I think it was like laser surgery, breaking up all the stones, because they've not been a problem to him since.

HE TOLD ME LATER
WHAT THE LORD SHOWED HIM

On the plane ride back from New Zealand, I sat with Randy. For about two hours, I poured out everything that I was relating to in all his stories of hunger, passion, being under the bondage of the demonic, finding freedom, and being used in healing. I shared my journey as God had dealt with my spirit of mammon. It seemed everything he talked about, I had lived and could relate to God's redeeming ways. I also got the chance to be very honest about my financial position and about the things in my past, so that there were no secrets. We haven't talked about it much but he has said he saw something in me that night that has encouraged me greatly, especially when the going got rough. It's something so big that I rarely talk about it in public, though.

By the time we got back to Los Angeles, I had decided I had to go with them to Toronto, which was the next trip. I had been worried about my finances, but now I was once again throwing caution to the wind - I just had to be there. I wanted so desperately to return to where I had been so wonderfully touched, where our marriage had been healed, and where I had such fond memories. If I had known how great it was going to be, I would never have thought about not going!

CHAPTER 6

TORONTO - BIRTH OF SO MUCH
IN RANDY AND ME

Randy, Ben and I met in Toronto on Tuesday night, October 7, 1998 for Randy to address about 350 pastors from around the world attending the pastor's conference prior to the start of "Catch the Fire." It was in meetings like this where Randy really shined. He had been on the verge of burn-out when God touched him before these four meetings in Toronto, so he knew exactly what pastors go through – he has a real heart for them. He has a real heart for them. The first night and next morning were about encouraging them, and he was very open and transparent about how dry he had been until just recently. He spoke about "pressing in," and while he had been speaking on this topic for some time, I was to see over the next year that it would become one of his major messages. He told one story that touched all of us: He had met a man recently who had been 18 when the 1948 healing revival had started. The man had just recently been to Toronto and had commented that he had to stand in line. As he stood in line, he had tears in his eyes as he realized that it had been 46 years since he had needed to stand in line to get into a church.

As Randy talked about humbling ourselves, about returning to intimate worship and contending for "more" of God, the anointing began to hit most in the room and many were crying, shaking, and even falling. The ministry time was wonderful, but it didn't stop there. The next morning he spoke from Acts 20 about how "God is looking for Fathers, not CEO's." I only heard him preach that message a few times while I traveled with him, but it's a great one and I wish everyone could hear it.

RANDY'S ASSOCIATES SHARE

At least 4000 packed the room for the opening night of the conference that Wednesday. The room was electric. It was so much fun being back there. I have to be honest - part of it was because of how special of a place it is to my wife and I, but also because this time I went with Randy Clark. I got to be on the ministry team, and I got a reserved seat and didn't have to get in line at 5 AM, as some did, to fight for a good seat. It was also special to be with people like Bill and Barbara Cassada, Charles and Anne Stock, Rick and Annie Stivers, and Bob Bradbury. These are people who have been associated with Randy's ministry and they all shared during the workshop Randy did that afternoon about how they had come to believe that "God can use little ole me." You could feel the faith increasing in this workshop of about one thousand. Ministry time was powerful, as Randy loosed us on everyone who wanted prayer.

GOD GAVE STORIES WE STILL TEACH TODAY

The next afternoon, Randy did another workshop, this time on words of knowledge for healing. I remember this workshop so vividly and have used these two examples in our teaching often. In the workshop, Randy taught on the six most common ways of recognizing words of knowledge, after which he prayed over the group. Then people who had never gotten words before were allowed to give them. It's amazing to see this gift de-mystified, and to watch the anointing come upon people as they get very detailed, accurate words for the first time.

One of the words was "gravel in the mouth." I've often said it was a good thing I wasn't allowed to interpret the word because my first thought was "It's about a speech impediment, like when they have to put marbles in your mouth to help you enunciate properly." That wasn't it at all. A man stood, said he had been surfing 10 years ago and was pushed by a wave into the sandy bottom. He had gotten "gravel in his mouth" and the force of the wave had wrenched his back causing back pain for 10 years. He knew the word was for him and, when he was prayed for, all the pain left! Another word was for a painful wrist. Three people responded to that word and went to a corner to be prayed for. Two left when nothing seemed to be happening, but the third said "I'm not leaving because I believe God wasn't just teasing here, and I want to get healed." That's exactly what happened - kinda says something about that "pressing in" thing I talked about earlier, huh?

THIS IS WHEN THE
BRAZILIAN CONNECTION WAS MADE!

Randy spoke on the final night of the conference and said it was going to be a night of explosions. That had already proven to be true. There was a group of about 100+ Brazilians who had come to the conference. At one point before the meeting, John Arnott, the Toronto church pastor, had invited Randy to come back into the hospitality room to talk with them. After a few minutes, Randy wanted to pray for them. When he got to the fifth one, as he raised his hand and began to say, "Come Holy Spirit," the power of God hit the Brazilian and he "crashed" to the floor. What they didn't know at the time was he had been an athlete, involved in an accident 10 years before that had left him unable to walk for a year while going through therapy, and that he now lived with constant back, leg, and neck pain. The pain had been so bad that morning that he had actually had tears in his eyes. He felt electricity go through him, and when he got up off the floor he realized all the pain was gone.

This made an impression on Randy, so he agreed to meet with the four Brazilian pastors who were insistent on meeting with him. When we finally got to meet with them, there were 30 pastors instead of four. This obvious display of hunger further impressed Randy.

At the time, we were preparing to meet with the rest of the Global Awakening team to pray about and discuss next year's schedule, and Randy already knew that he didn't have room on his calendar to fit them in for 1999. There were several different denominations represented by that group, however, and particularly prevalent was a group sent by the headquarters church of the Foursquare denomination in Sao Paulo to bring back someone to help spark revival in Brazil. Randy was also particularly taken with a Baptist pastor from Belo Horizonte. Shortly after that meeting, everything fell into place for us to go in March 1999, first to Cordoba, Argentina (this was the series of meetings I was originally scheduled to go to back in June 1998 – I got to go after all!), and then on to Sao Paulo and Belo Horizonte.

THE GOLD DUST

Several days after the conference in Toronto, Carol and I flew into Providence, Rhode Island to attend some meetings at a church pastored by Lance Wallnau and to attend the Global Awakening meetings. This was our first chance to meet with the various people associated with Randy's ministry. People from Randy's church and the Global Awakening office were there - Gail, who ran the office, Bill and Helen, who oversaw the intercessory prayer, Bill and Barbara from New Jersey, who were a resource team, and Bill Johnson from the church in Redding. Charles and Anne Stock, pastors of a church in Harrisburg, PA where Randy was to ultimately locate his ministry 3 years later, were there. Bob Bradbury, the commercial fisherman who had caught for Randy in a meeting and had "caught" the anointing attended, as did Richard and Glenda Holcolmb, Richard being Randy's chief intercessor from Texas. They were great meetings, and we got to see firsthand the high caliber of people who were associated with this organization.

There were always "interesting" things happening, like the time after the morning meeting when we went to an adjacent room to have lunch. Charles' face was sprinkled with gold specks. We kidded him about getting into some child's glitter packet, and Ben said jokingly, "Oh, it must be some of that gold dust we heard about in Toronto." Someone had come to Randy while we were there and had told him about being in a meeting with the woman from Brazil who had gold dust pouring from her hair. We had been very skeptical then, and we did not quite believe it. Even when Charles washed it all off and it all reappeared on his face, we continued to pooh-pooh it. Little did we know how soon we would see it up close and personal.

THE ARGENTINE REVIVALISTS

After four days of being in meetings and with the Global Awakening team, Carol flew home and Randy, Ben and I flew down to Buenos Aires, Argentina for a pastor's conference. I had finally made it to Argentina! The meetings were to be held at Del Centro Baptist Church, co-pastored by Dr. Carlos Maraida and Dr. Pablo Deiros. This is the oldest Baptist church in Argentina and is more Pentecostal than most of the churches that claim to be charismatic or Pentecostal in the US. There were about 1500 pastors and leaders from all over Latin America; Randy was to do the night meetings, and Carlos Anacondia would lead the first afternoon meeting. In fact, we arrived at our hotel, which was within walking distance of the church, freshened up just a bit and got over to the that meeting. Carlos was just beginning to speak. He and Randy had developed a deep friendship over the past few years, and we got to spend some time with him afterwards in the hospitality room. I have to admit, I was pinching myself as I realized that I was sitting in a room with three of the leaders of the Argentine revival (Deiros, Maraida, and Annacondia). My theory was: get their hands on me, and something was bound to rub off. We were all able to get prayer from Carlos, as well as from Deiros and Maraida. I had never heard of them, but what godly, scholarly men they are, and how respected they are in their church and the seminary where they both teach.

RANDY DOES THE NIGHT MEETINGS

That night, Randy was the speaker. The atmosphere was electric. There were all these pastors and leaders from all over Latin America. They came hungry, and God came ready to heal. We saw a lot happen just from the words of knowledge, and many were standing as soon as Randy or Ben gave a word for healing, completely healed. There was such faith just in the releasing of the word. Randy had many come to the platform to testify what had happened to them.

One of the stories that stands out to me even now is of this one woman who came up with much improved hearing in one ear as a result of the word. But she still couldn't hear out of the other ear. As Randy was interviewing those who came across the platform, he just had her stand there as he put his hand on her ear. We always teach to give the person you're praying for your complete attention, but everything is still to be guided by the Holy Spirit, and in this case He had told Randy to just pray for her. After about 10 testimonies, she could hear out of that ear!

After Randy's message we prayed until early in the morning. And by "we," I mean Randy, Ben and I, praying for 1500 people. I know there were other pastors praying, but they mostly wanted us to pray – like we had...something. I can understand them lining up for Randy, but they thought Ben and I had something just because we were Anglos and working with Randy. I was thinking, "I need you Argentines and Brazilians to pray for me – you're the guys who know about revival!"

CLAUDIO AND I LOOK ALIKE - SORT OF

The next afternoon Claudio Freidzon was the speaker. I was really excited because I had heard so much about him, but I had never been in a meeting with him. We followed Randy in to be positioned along the front row (a definite perk of traveling with Randy). Both Claudio and his wife, Betty, spoke and the message was great. Then he said he was going to pray for everyone. The chairs were quickly stacked and we were on the front row as Claudio came down from the platform. There was a warm smile of recognition as he approached Randy, and then he acknowledged Ben and me. We all received prayer, and they got us up again just to knock us right back over. Then he got us again as we passed by to go back to the hospitality room! Randy often told the story of being prayed for by Benny Hinn and trying to tell him, "I want what Claudio Freidzon got" but he was so drunk he couldn't say the words and finally had to blurt out "I want what the Argentine got." I just kept hoping I got even just a little of what Claudio has – after all, we look very much alike, what with the same hairstyle (or lack thereof).

WE WENT TO SEE OMAR!

Randy spoke again that night and it was pretty much a blowout. As we started the third day, I was really excited because the afternoon speaker was Sergio Scataglini, and none of us had met him. We didn't get to meet or even see him, however. Instead, they arranged for us to go see Omar Cabrera and pray for his wife. Omar was one of the original leaders of the Argentine revival. Randy had found favor with him several years earlier when he had come to Argentina to learn more about the revival that he was being identified with. I had read about Omar in books by Peter Wagner and others. The man and what he did in Argentina for the Body of Christ was stunning, and there we were, sitting on his couch in his living room, talking and then praying for and receiving prayer from him! Marta, his wife, had recently had something like a stroke, but they felt like it was a demonic attack upon her. We got to talk with both of them and pray for her. I wish I could say it all had a happy conclusion, but she died several months later.

WE WERE MADE FOR THIS

After getting back to the hotel and getting something to eat, we got ready for the evening and walked back to the church at 9pm, thinking Randy would come in right as they were finishing worship and ready to begin teaching. What we found was a sanctuary in chaos, with bodies everywhere and chairs still stacked up. Sergio had ministered after his afternoon message and it had just kept going. They had just carried him out as we arrived - literally. He is known for bringing the "fire of holiness of God" and that's what had happened. They put the sanctuary back together quickly as we waited, praying for the sick they brought out to us in the courtyard.

After Randy's message, we ministered for roughly 4 hours, well into the wee hours of the morning. We came back on Sunday morning for him to preach, but he never did. They wanted him to bless the little kids before coming into the service, but Randy can't just say a simple blessing and leave it at that. He ended up praying over every single child, the teachers, and the mothers, and there were a lot. We walked into the main sanctuary just as Dr. Maraida was finishing his message, which God had given him during worship. So, we entered into ministry time, altogether another 4 hours. As I had it figured, we had gone 16 hours without eating, and we had been on our feet ministering for 8 of those hours.

I've had this revelation on several occasions before, but it was then than I realized again: "I WAS BORN FOR THIS!" We were taken to lunch for some great Argentine beef, with the added bonus that we got to sit with a man who had been the administrative man for Carlos Annacondia for many years as he was first getting started doing crusades in Latin America. He told us many stories, but the one that stood out to us was the story about the one time they had to limit the testimonies about teeth getting gold filings to those who had received no less than five. So many people were getting gold teeth in the meetings that anything less than five was no longer a big deal. Wow! After a little shopping, we flew back to the US to Oklahoma City, where Randy was to start a conference with Drs. Deiros and Maraida, and Pablo Bottari, who was the deliverance minister for Annacondia for 11 years. He's the man who had developed the deliverance model that Randy's ministry was embracing.

MY INTRODUCTION TO FIBROMYALGIA

The church was located in Edmunds, a suburb of Oklahoma City. The Argentineans and I were staying at a mansion, while Randy and Ben were staying at the pastor's house. That night, they gave a big dinner for us before Randy would go teach on prayer ministry to equip the prayer team who would help during the conference. I was particularly drawn to Jean, who was a lovely white haired lady in her 50s. She told me she had suffered with debilitating pain for about five years; the diagnosis was fibromyalga. She was in so much pain that day she almost didn't come, but she was determined not to miss this opportunity to sit under Randy's ministry. After the teaching that night, I got to pray for her. I don't know how it happened - I didn't come against any spirit, but she "rested in the Spirit" for a long while and when she got up, all the pain was gone. We've since learned that there's usually a spirit behind that disease. All I know is, for the next five days, she literally beamed. She simply glowed. She was so excited that she had no pain and that she was being used so powerfully in ministry.

GOLD DUST — UP CLOSE AND PERSONAL

Now, remember how I talked earlier in this chapter about how we were going to encounter this "gold dust thing" up close and personal? It turned out that Ruth Ward Heflin had come to the conference as an attendee. Randy knew her and trusted her ministry. During the conference, Randy would have some of the pastors come to an upstairs dining room to have lunch with him and the team, and he would talk and answer any questions they might have. They would always ask about the revival in Latin America and, after telling a few stories of what he had been seeing, he turned to Ruth and said, "I understand you've had an experience from Brazil. Would you tell us about it?" As she proceeded to relate how she had met the woman from Brazil who had gold dust falling from her hair, both Randy and I noticed that gold dust was forming all over Ruth. We couldn't believe it! Then she opened up her Bible and showed everyone how it accumulated on the pages. I noticed she had turned to Psalm 110 and I asked her if that was of any significance. "Oh no," she said, "it's all through my bible," and as she flipped the pages, gold dust flew everywhere. Randy actually ran his finger across one page and it left a clean mark like your finger would going across a very dusty table. We were really sorry to leave, but I had to pull Randy out of the meeting so he could go do a radio interview.

Later we found out she had offered to pray for everyone, and soon the room had been littered with 30 pastor's and leader's bodies. One young man from this church had been secretly crying out to God: "I want to speak your word with anointing and power." Not knowing any of this, she leaned over him as he rested on the floor and said something like, "God shows me you will speak His word with authority." Ben and everyone else in the room testified that his mouth was ringed with gold flakes! It didn't stop there. Ruth left the conference after this luncheon, as planned, and no one in the conference knew about what had happened during this small lunch meeting. Two nights later, on the last night of the conference, Randy called me over to look at something just as I was going to check on the book table around midnight. There was a woman with a black pantsuit who had gold dust all over her. You could even see the outline of a handprint on one of her pant legs. I didn't know this until later, but she was from a Church of Christ, a denomination that doesn't even believe in any of this charismatic stuff - yet there she was, covered with gold dust that *we* didn't even believe in a few weeks before. All she knew was that she was feeling the presence of God in a way she never had before.

After receiving a financial blessing from our hosts (this is part of their ministry and the 8 of us who stayed there all received this blessing), I flew home to San Diego. I had been gone 16 days from Carol. It's often been said there's a cost to the anointing, and I can attest to this being true. The best way I can describe it is that I had been in rarified air during that time in Argentina and being around the Argentineans in the US conference. Something had rubbed off. For the next three days, Carol would shake violently anytime I got near her. When we went to bed at night, I would have to leave the room until she fell asleep because she would shake the bed so much. So 16 days turned into 19 - there is a cost to the anointing.

CHAPTER 7

NOVEMBER & DECEMBER MEETINGS
PRODUCE LASTING STORIES

November's meeting was in San Jose, at a church called The Father's House, where we did 5 days of meetings. It wasn't often that Randy would start meetings like this with deliverance, but that's what he did. In fact, there was a lot of deliverance during those meetings. It was during this time that Carol received her anointing for deliverance ministry, through the "baptism under fire." She had come with me for these meetings, and she found out firsthand those two terrible things an associate of Randy's can hear during a meeting. You know the ones I mean – the first is the over call the microphone during ministry time. It goes like this: Randy says, "Carol, can you come over here for a second?" It means he's stirred up something and he wants you to handle it. The second is to feel a tap on your shoulder while ministering and someone says, "Randy sent me," and they're twitching and growling. Carol was called on many times during the next 5 days for deliverance. Now, in our equipping sessions, she comments that she started by literally reading of the Ten Steps for Deliverance sheet, trying to read in a dimly lit room without her glasses. It was still effective in achieving freedom for that person, however, and she got a love for this ministry and for seeing people set free in the process.

THE MEETINGS PRODUCE GREAT STORIES

During one of the afternoon meetings, a blind young man named Chris was brought into the meeting. He had never been in church before, but he gave his life to the Lord. The man who led him said it was so easy, that he totally understood that you have to walk by faith and not sight. He received a lot of prayer that afternoon and evening. He developed tear ducts, which he had been born without, and his eyes had turned from white to blue. He still couldn't see, but the local church people were going to stay in contact with him and pray for him. At the end of the evening, he sat down beside a woman. She took his hand. As soon as she did, all the pain she had been feeling all day suddenly left - a healing anointing had been placed upon him.

We also got to minister to the Hispanic church that meets there. About 800 came for an afternoon meeting. It was the first time Randy had ministered at a Hispanic church in the US. He told many stories of the things he had seen in Latin America, explaining that it wasn't just for there, but for here as well. He told of the meeting in Central America where the backslidden young man prayed for his mother, who had a cancerous tumor. When Randy had a word for it, she fell to the ground trembling, and her son prayed because there weren't enough prayer team members to pray for everyone. The tumor shrank under his hand! The next day, he and his sister gave their lives back to the Lord.

At another meeting in Argentina, a businessman who was on the team from the US prayed for a man who was blind and deaf in one eye and ear. He realized what a skeptic he was when the man was healed in front of him and he still had a hard time accepting it. I'll admit this was a wake-up call for me not to get complacent. In the four months I had thus far traveling with Randy, I had seen so much and had gotten used to believing that we were going to see signs and wonders regularly. But there were always plenty of people in the meetings who were new to all of this, and there were some who just couldn't believe. I realized I needed to love them and pray for their eyes to be opened. I haven't stopped since then.

RANDY'S ROOTS

While November's meeting had been relatively close to our home, December's meetings were close to Randy's home. The first meetings were in a small town called Streator, Illinois, and the second set were in Marion, Illinois. The meetings in Streator were held in an armory which could hold about 1000 people - unfortunately, only about 137 showed up. It didn't seem to matter, though; the anointing was still very present.

The meetings at Friendly Regional Church of God in Marion, Illinois were like a homecoming for Randy. He had grown up in the area, and the Baptist church he had first pastored was right down the road. We even got to meet many of the friends we had heard him tell stories about. The first night was for training of the prayer team that would be functioning for these meetings. As Randy taught on healing and recognizing words of knowledge for healing, he was dropping nuggets of wisdom everywhere. One of the things he recommended while interviewing was to ask the person what is going with their body, but not to let them give so much information that it sucks the faith out of you. He also told them that they can pray all the way home after they get healed, but during the prayer he just wants them to concentrate on their body so that they will know what God is doing. We always tell them, "It's hard to drink and talk at the same time." We Pentecostals and charismatics tend to want to pray in tongues as soon as we start getting prayed for.

I STIRRED UP A HORNET'S NEST

Randy also told them to be direct, pray for effect, find out what God is doing, and bless that. If God is moving on someone, keep praying. This was all good teaching and the prayer team ate it up. As I wrote the report about these training sessions, however, I stirred up a swirl of controversy.

I wrote all the reports of Randy's meetings. They were sent to the Global Awakening email list and to the New Wine list, a large list for those who were interested in the renewal. There was a time when there would be perhaps 30 posts a day, especially for about a week before a major Toronto conference or a conference at Harvest Rock in Pasadena, CA. These would be followed by numerous posts afterwards recounting how great the conference had been. One of the signs of a "been there, done that" attitude that has pervaded the American church for the past few years is that this list has become almost dormant. But when I stated, "We have recently been reading a series of books about William Branham. While he was off some theologically, he was probably the most anointed man used by God for healing in America. Reading about him has encouraged all of us on Randy's team that we need to be pressing in for more, that there's so much more that God has for us," it stirred up a hornet's nest. Ben was checking the mail when he started coming across all these posts about my comments. It seems that one person had taken exception to my even talking about Branham, called him a "false prophet" and tried to raise suspicion against Randy for talking about him. Many, many people came to our defense but it wasn't pleasant to see what you had written being dissected by 50+ people over the next few days. It did, however, give me a glimpse into what Randy had endured from the opponents of the "Toronto Blessing," who attacked him in print and over the radio.

THE FEAR OF MAN REARS ITS HEAD

When I had first started traveling with Randy, he had told me, "If you get a word of knowledge come on up and give it," not realizing I didn't move regularly in that gift. That night I had a specific word, but I was afraid to give it. This was not an unusual occurrence – many times I would have someone come up to me at the end of a meeting and say, "I had a word tonight, but I was afraid to give it." I would write in the report, "Oh, how the fear of man keeps us from doing the things of God."

That night it became very clear to me that I was also talking about myself. I couldn't give the word I got that night because I was afraid, afraid of being wrong or looking stupid in front of Randy and Ben. I've used that example many times now to break the fear that people naturally have when stepping out in this gift. I think the important part is to remember that someone will get healed if you're right, not that you might look stupid or give a wrong word. That right there, when someone gets healed because you gave the word, is worth any embarrassment you might feel if you were wrong or no one responded. To make sure I got the point that night, Randy had the word I had gotten and I watched a young man get healed instantly when it was released. And to make sure I really got it, God arranged for him to be my catcher for the night! Okay, message received.

As God continued to give me stories for the future, one of the men on the prayer team prayed for one of the pastor's daughters at the end of the meeting. He prayed for her to receive all the gifts of the Spirit and to be anointed for healing. Down she went in the Spirit, where she stayed for about 30 minutes - she was still in a daze an hour later when we all went to get something to eat. Now, Randy always talks about the "impartation" that happens in these meetings, that you can actually get a great anointing through the laying on of hands. It's the stirring up of that gift that is talked about in 1 and 2 Timothy, the gift which is given by God but which is brought into fuller activation through the power of the Holy Spirit working through the laying on of hands. I watched this young woman the next night as she was praying for everyone who moved. She told me she felt a new confidence and boldness and she was moving in greater clarity for words of knowledge and in the healing anointing. Wow, she got it!

On the last night of the meetings, God gave me two more stories that I use today. A woman came up to me and asked if I remembered praying for her back pain two nights before. I did and I remembered that all the pain had left. She asked me why I had prayed something about her eyes, since she hadn't said anything about them, and I vaguely remembered that some words had just come tumbling out about her eyes but I hadn't known why. She told me she had just come from her eye doctor - she had been having spots before her eyes and he had told her that she was going to have to have an operation. Their appointment was to confirm the operation for the next week, but when he checked her one last time he couldn't find any spots and canceled the operation! I had moved in one of the ways of receiving words of knowledge for healing, inspired speech, which occurs when a word just come out, one that you hadn't intended to say. Inspired words just just come flowing forth. When I released the words I had said about her eyes during my prayer for her back, she was instantly healed!

YOU WOULD NEVER KNOW
I WAS DOING DELIVERANCE

At the end of this night, during the ministry time, one of the men on the prayer team came to me concerning ministry he needed. He had been a Christian for about 25 years, in deliverance ministry for 12 years, but was struggling in one area of his life. Occasionally he would fall into looking at pornography – he had been introduced to Playboy magazine when he was about 12 years old. He would repent, would confess it to his pastor and his wife, but every once in a while he would fall, feeling like he had no control, as though he were being pushed over a cliff by a bulldozer. That's the way the demonic works. I didn't feel like I was to make a big deal of this, and that I was to go and get some more prayer ministers and take him off to a private place. I think the Lord was setting me up so I would have this story for later.

We just sat on the back of the pew as the rest of the 800+ people were in full blown renewal, many down in the Spirit, laughing or shaking, and some getting healing prayer. If you had walked by us at that point, you would have never known I was doing deliverance on him. You would have thought I was just blessing him, as I quietly prayed for him. I led him in renouncing his binding with that spirit, using a quiet but authoritative voice. One of the things we teach in our deliverance equipping is that the devil is not impressed with our volume, but he's scared to death by our relationship and intimacy with God. As we got to the point when I commanded the Spirit to come up and out on the breath, he just sighed heavily. I asked him what, if anything, had happened, and he said he felt something leave him and that he felt lighter.

At this point in the story, my left-brained, analytical side usually wants to know if this is actually real, and one of the advantages of my position with Randy's ministry was that I got to write these reports and interview the people. In this case I was able to stay in contact with this man for a year and a half. He continued to tell me that he no longer had the problem he had had with pornography and that he was truly free. I use this story to illustrate that you can do this ministry anywhere and it usually doesn't look like Linda Blair receiving ministry in the movie "The Exorcist." You need to be ready and equipped in season and out, but this ministry really works to get someone free so they can stay that way.

SHE CAME IN ON
CRUTCHES SHE CARRIED THEM OUT

As we were wrapping up that night, I got another blessing. We had moved many people into the gym, since there wasn't enough room for everyone during ministry time in the sanctuary. Randy had been in there, going down the line praying for people. I had noticed him praying for a woman named Kay for a couple of minutes. We had seen her come into the meeting, moving very slowly and painfully on crutches. She didn't need healing – she needed an overhaul. She had pain in her neck, shoulders, arms, back, legs, and knees. I came over to relieve Randy so he could move on down the line and pray for others. As I started praying for Kay, she started feeling the power of God. Heat came into her shoulders and then down her back. I prayed for the "oil of the Spirit" to flow and it was as though it was seeping into all the painful areas, taking the pain out. She wanted to attempt to walk without her crutches, and while we did tell her to not do anything to hurt herself, we did put two men on each side of her as she began taking some steps. You could see the anointing get stronger as she began to walk with confidence. As I prayed some more, she went down under the power and my catchers and I left her there, laughing and having a great time. I wasn't sure what God had done until later. She came walking back into the sanctuary, thanked me for the prayer and walked briskly out of the church – carrying her crutches!

I MET THE PERSON IN THE STORY

One other blessing of these meetings was to meet Heather Harvey. She was 19 at the time, but she was 14 when she came to Toronto to receive her healing. I had seen her testimony on one of the videos from Toronto, so I knew a little about her, but now, once again, my little left brain, analytical, even somewhat skeptical side got to see the results of prayer. You see, while I have believed in prayer for healing since I got touched in 1992, there is also a part of me that wants to know that it's real, and not just emotional. It might be real for a day or a week, but does it stay?

Heather was severely dyslexic. School, and life, was very hard. Reading anything was an extreme chore. She and her family had been in Toronto for meetings in the early days of Toronto, and had been prayed for by Randy. On their last night there before driving home to Kentucky, they asked him if he would pray one more time. Randy told them he still had some to pray for who had not been prayed for yet, but if they could wait he would pray again. Randy often says the anointing goes up after 11 – those are the times when you see who's the most desperate. They were.

Finally, after about an hour, Randy prayed for Heather again. This time she lay perfectly still on the floor, not like the other times he had prayed for her. When she came to, about 45 minutes later, she told her mother she had had a vision of angels operating on her brain, rewiring her. They brought her a Bible - she could read perfectly! But the story doesn't stop there. After driving some 17 hours home through a snowstorm, she went immediately over to her best friend's house. Walking right up to her, without saying anything at all about what had happened to her in Toronto, she just laid hands on her and claimed that God was going to heal her. The friend had dyslexia as well, and while she was on the ground for about 45 minutes, the same thing happened – she had a vision of angels operating on her, rewiring the brain. When she got up, her dyslexia was gone.

On that December night in Marion, Heather was testifying on how God had healed her, and how she had recently graduated from high school, 5th in her class. Oh, and guess who has a healing anointing and sees God do miracles everywhere she goes?

These were the last meetings of the year 1998. We now had 4 weeks off to enjoy the holidays and prepare to go to Colombia in early January. It was to be a significant trip for all of us who went. I didn't know it at the time, but God was giving me a test and, thankfully, this time I passed it.

CHAPTER 8

THE SACRIFICE WAS SO WORTH IT

By the time December rolled around, it was painfully obvious that the support money I was receiving wasn't enough to continue traveling with Randy. I was faced with a decision – either stop traveling and go to work, or sell the one asset we had left, our 1993 Lexus ES300. This was a huge battle for me. Now, I know not everyone will understand this, but I loved that car. I had bought it brand new, it was now paid for, and it was a beautiful red with grey underclading. That they no longer made that color made it even more special. It was the last vestige of my old life, and I had always maintained that I wouldn't sell that car because if I went back to work we would need two cars and I would need to have a "good" car.

In hindsight I can see that God had to see just how desperate I was for Him. I had one foot in His world, but I still wanted things my way, still wanted a way out in case this "ministry thing" didn't work out.

Very, very reluctantly I put the car up for sale before I went out on the road for the December trip. When Carol called one night and said that someone had come to test drive the car and said they were intending to buy it, I thought, "at least God's sparing my feelings and having Carol do the deal while I'm gone – that's nice at least." The car didn't sell then or the rest of December, however, and I thought, "Maybe He was just testing me to see if I would be obedient, maybe I don't have to sell my car – maybe He's going to provide another way." That's what I wanted to believe, but there wasn't peace in my spirit. I put the car up for sale again in early January,

1999. It immediately sold at the price I was asking. I have to admit, there was some sadness as I watched it drive away, but at least I now had enough money to continue traveling. We would now be content with driving a 10 year old Honda as our only car. Once again, not a big deal for many people – but it was not what I had been used to and it was huge for me. God was breaking me.

Through all this, an interesting thing happened in Columbia. One night, as Ben and I were praying for Randy before one of the meetings, I suddenly got a pain in my wrist, followed by a pain in my leg and down to my foot. Those pains really hurt! Randy began laughing and I said, "Is this what it's like to get words by feeling the pain?" He said, "Yep, you got it." While I had gotten a few words of knowledge before, I had never gotten them by feeling the pain in my body, something Randy moved in 95% of the time - the anointing had rubbed off just by being around him. And you will never convince me that the selling of the car wasn't directly related to this anointing coming on me. God honors sacrifice and obedience and He saw my hunger.

AN APOSTOLIC LEADER

This was the first trip that we took with other people on the team. Randy brought two of his associates from the church in St. Louis, a missionary to Africa, his chief intercessor, Ben and myself. The trip had been set up by a connection through Charles Stock, and there were to be two people that Randy would get to meet.

The first stop was in Bogotá to do two nights of meetings. The highlight was the chance to have an interview with Cesear Castellanos, who pastored the fastest growing church in the world at that time, Mision Carismatica Internacional. We had heard stories of this man and how God was using him in Colombia to build a church based on cells, groups of 12. One of the things they do there and in other parts of Latin America is to get new converts to an "encounter weekend" as soon as they are saved. There, the leaders make sure they are truly saved, get baptized in the Spirit, are led through inner healing and deliverance, and are given a vision of the church. When they come back from one of these weekends they are on fire for the Lord and, consequently, stay in the church, becoming an integral part of the growth and vision of the church.

The statistics tells us that only 4-6% of those who were invited to give their lives to the Lord at a crusade in the US are still in the church a year later. In Argentina, that rate is 85%. Randy once asked Carlos Annacondia why this was so. He said, "In North America you give them enough of the Gospel to get them saved, but not enough to get them set free."

It was interesting to hear this man's perspective on the incredible growth of his church, which had grown by 100,000 while he was out of the country recuperating from gunshot wounds one year. He told us that they had 27,000 cells and each averaged 10 people. In 2000, I read a book which studied his church. It said the church membership had grown to 350,000 and was growing exponentially every day. It was an honor to meet him, and Randy was thrilled. It got even better - Cesear changed his plans the next night by inviting Randy and his two associates to join him for dinner. Randy commented later that he was a little unnerved when he noticed the bulletproof jackets under the seats in the limousine that came to pick them up. This is a very dangerous country and Cesear has been targeted by the drug cartels, so he had to take precautions.

LIKE HOT WAX HAD
BEEN POURED ON HER HANDS!

After two days in Bogata, we flew to Medellin to do 6 days of meetings, primarily at a church under the apostolic leadership of Randy MacMillan. Randy is an American who has been down there for about 30 years. The pastor he has in Medellin is Andrew McMillan (no relation), who is also an American and had been there about 20 years. I think we all had a sense these were going to be powerful meetings. Richard, Randy's chief intercessor from Texas, had previously had two dreams exactly alike about angelic visitation, and felt that the ministry here would be very easy.

When we got to the hotel, Andrew arranged for us to meet with his leadership, about 20 people. After Randy shared some, he prophesied over a few and prayed for them all. At one point, I felt I was to go pray for a young woman who was sitting on the floor. As I just touched the palm of her hand, the fire of God hit her - literally. She started shaking her hands like they hurt, and started running around the room. It was a hotel meeting room, and they had provided pitchers of ice cold water for us. She ran to the table and dumped two pitchers over her head to cool herself off. It looked strange indeed but over the next few days, the leadership of the church said she prophesied more accurately than ever before and there seemed to be a new anointing on her. We were off to a good start!

BEN TRANSLATES — AND GETS HEALED

That first night, Friday, was youth night. The 300 youth of that church were joined by youth groups from several other churches as well as some of the main body of adults. 1,800 people were packed into the church that night. Ben proved invaluable to Randy in Latin America, as he had spent 7 years in Guatemala and spoke Spanish fluently. We got our first taste of the hunger in Colombia when Randy gave an altar call that night. He had been told, "You won't think they have understood you when you give a call for salvation and rededication because so many will come up." This proved to be the case as 300 came forward, 35 of whom gave their lives to the Lord for the first time!

There is a great move of repentance going on in Colombia. We even got to see God's healing power on one of the team members. I wrote in my report that, "Ben had come with an infected ear (maybe God's way of saying one earring was enough) and it was painful to even touch. During the night, God sovereignly healed him and it no longer hurt at all to touch his ear." Being boys at heart, we hit him on the ear several times to make sure he was still healed.

In the morning meeting the next day, Randy went for words of knowledge for healing, as usual. 65 people indicated that they had been healed. He had just started back up to the platform when he felt a very severe pain in his knee. One thing we've noticed is that the more severe the pain is, the higher the number of people who will be healed of that pain.

Randy called all who had knee pain up and 50 responded. Within 5 minutes of releasing us and the prayer team from the church, there were 25 who were healed. I prayed for one of our translators, who got immediately healed. She reached down to the young woman next to her, commanded all the pain to be gone as I had just done, and she was also healed - talk about giving it away! And this was typical of these meetings: we would start at 10 AM and walk out of there at 2:30 to go get lunch. But the true heroes of that day were Ben and John, the missionary with us. They stayed another 2 hours ministering deliverance to a young man. They said it was all worth it - he walked out free in the Spirit!

STORIES OF HEALING

The meeting that Saturday night was one of the most powerful and anointed nights Randy said he had ever experienced, and Pastor Andrew said it was the most powerful night his church had ever experienced. It actually started about an hour before the meeting. Randy and I were in the hotel room talking when he suddenly arched backwards, then doubled over and yelled in pain. It was a very severe word of knowledge and Randy knew God wanted to do something significant that night. I just needed to remind him not to forget it. After Randy took some testimonies, he felt it was time to release the word. At least 150 people stood in response to that word. Others stood as he gave a few other words. When he finished praying over them for healing, he took the count as usual by having them wave both arms over their heads until their wrists crossed. It looked like windmills going all over the room as 159 indicated they had been healed! Since we had just dramatically witnessed the power of God, he gave an altar call for salvation and rededication. This time 125 responded, 48 for the first time. So much happened that night that I actually had to write another report. Randy says the anointing goes up after 11 and you often see the most dramatic healings then because it's the desperate who will stay; you know there's desperation in the room when the service starts at 6PM and we didn't leave until 12:30, and there were still a lot of people there. There are many stories I could tell of that evening, but I will share these three.

During the prayer call for anointing for healing, a young man came forward. He fell under the power of God and the fire of God came on his hands. They became contracted, were icy cold, and stayed like this for 4 hours. This was the same thing that happened to Randy when Rodney Howard Browne prayed for him in Florida right before Toronto broke out. The pastor said this young man had only been coming to his church for about a year and was only lukewarm. Once again God shows it's not about our works - it's His grace when He chooses us and anoints us.

Randy prayed quite awhile for a woman who needed an overhaul. When he needed to move on to pray for others, he called me over to continue praying for her. She had received a lot of healing already and I concentrated on her knees and legs. She had no circulation, experienced a great deal of pain, and she had a lot of trouble walking. As I prayed for her, the heat that had been in her body now moved to the legs. I had a picture of us walking in an oval and that as she stepped out in faith the anointing would get stronger and stronger. She wanted to try it, but could only take two baby steps at a time at first. She was laboring to even lift up her legs. As I continued to pray, the anointing started to kick in and she started walking more briskly. I won't say she was dragging me around, but almost. We watched her walk out of the meeting like she had never had a problem.

Meanwhile, Randy had begun praying for a young woman with cerebral palsy who had been born completely deaf in both ears. She could only communicate by sign language. When she felt heat, Randy was encouraged. When she thought she could hear, Randy had her close her eyes and he began snapping his fingers near her ears. When she indicated she could hear that, he had everyone around start praying. Then he said, "The next voice you hear will be your mother's." She was standing behind her, the girl had her eyes closed, and as the mother called "Astrid-Vanessa" the girl smiled and pointed to herself. Others would call out her name and she would point towards the sound. When the shout of the people went up to give glory to God, you could have heard it all over the neighborhood.

CHANGED FOREVER

You never know how someone's life is going to be impacted by one of these meetings. On Sunday morning Randy was off ministering to the children before the morning service. Andrew's wife, Cathy, had everyone stretch their hands toward the children's building to bless them. The keyboard player, Paoula, who was the daughter of the associate pastor, was overcome by the Spirit and had to be helped off the platform - she shook for the rest of the meeting. While she was in ministry leadership, she said she had been going through the motions. God had put a burden for the children in her up on that platform, however. She had recently transferred to that department and now God had put His anointing on it. God empowered her for "more" and all through the rest of the week people would fall under the power of God as soon as she touched them, something that had not been happening before. Today, she and her husband (one of the other translators) oversee the children's ministry of this church.

The power of God was so strong in that meeting. At one point, Ben prayed for a 2 year old baby with pneumonia. The child cried the whole time. When Ben cursed the sickness, the baby gagged and turned purple. Ben quickly told the afflicting spirit to leave, and the baby coughed, then went out in the Spirit for 20 minutes. While it had scared Ben and the mother both to see the baby turn purple, he said it was one of the most dramatic healings he had seen – and all in less than two minute!

MONDAY & TUESDAY
MORNING MEETINGS — PACKED OUT!

A small pastor's meeting had been arranged to be held at a local charismatic church on Monday morning. Andrew, our host, told us he didn't know how many people would show up, but it might only be about 20. Imagine our surprise when we walked into a church filled to capacity at 10 AM on a Monday morning – some 500 people! I kept thinking, "Oh God, do it in America." Randy didn't get the platform until 11:30, and only one-fourth of the people had left by the time we left at 3:30. There was such a hunger in this country.

Interestingly, at one point there was an altar call for salvation and rededication. Logic said that only committed Christians would be at church on a Monday morning, but 58 came forward, half confessing Jesus for the first time. One of the things that blessed us most in this meeting was to see an impartation for healing come upon the young people who had been assigned to the team to translate for us. My translator, Xiomara, got particularly touched that day; the fire of God fell on her and she shook all day long. I encouraged her to pray for others in my place, and you could see the Spirit flow through her. I have talked to her several times since by email. She is in love with Jesus and still flows in the healing anointing.

RANDY FELT LIKE A TARGET

The next two nights we did meetings in a square outside of one of the roughest sections of Medellin called Bello. I guess it's all relative, since we were in what was known at that time as the kidnap and murder capital of the world. Still, we knew this was different when we were getting out of the van and Cathy told us, "Don't stray from the group – we've had some trouble with knifings in the past." Despite this, we never felt as though we were in danger while we were in Columbia. Randy did have his moment, though. The youth pastor had told him this story:

> *One of the kids had confessed that he was "backslidden." Now, you normally think it would probably be about sex or drugs - normal teenager things. This kid, however, had been a paid assassin and his backsliding was a little more serious! He got paid a certain amount for these jobs, but he said, "I'd kill gringos for free." As Randy stood in the spotlight that night, he had to fight off the thought, "I'm a target!!" It wasn't until we were back that we started to understand how dangerous this country really is for Christians and Americans in particular.*

> *In any event, we had two great nights of meetings in this plaza; each night we had about 2500 people attend. On the first night, Randy and Ben gave words of knowledge for healing and within 15 minutes we had 244 healed in the first wave. Notice I said "first." Following this, Randy gave an altar call for salvation or rededication and 175 responded. He then went for deliverance and at least 100 were taken off to the special area set aside for just such a purpose. Since the people had now seen the power of God to heal, save and deliver, Randy gave another altar call and another 65 gave their lives to the Lord! Another wave of healing hit and 40 more were healed. Amazingly, the same thing happened the next night, and the numbers were even higher! One of the great stories we took from those meetings happened to Richard. He said he will never forget the tears of joy from a mother of a small child as he prayed for his crossed eyes to be straight and they were instantly healed.*

MINISTER WITH EYES WIDE OPEN

From Medellin, we moved on to Cali, where we went into Randy MacMillin's church with Andrew accompanying us. As Carol and I have now taught on prayer ministry for the past few years, I have used this story to emphasize the importance of "keeping your eyes open while you pray." One of the leaders in this church, who had only been a Christian for a short while, was praying for a woman with his eyes closed and no catcher. I was too far away to do anything as I watched in horror as she went straight back like a board onto the very thin carpet on the hard concrete floor. She hurt her neck and ear and had a huge bump on the back of her head. After some prayer, her neck and ear pain went away, but she still had a big bump and pain in her head. She had some anger toward the man who had prayed for her so I led her in renouncing her anger and un-forgiveness, and had her pray to bless the man. About that time the man just "happened" to walk up to her (coincidence? hmmmm). He apologized, she forgave him, they embraced, and both began speaking in tongues and sort of collapsed on the floor. She told me later she had absolutely no pain, although there was still a large bump.

There are a lot of lessons here: don't pray with your eyes closed, make sure you're looking out for the safety of the person receiving prayer (it's a myth that if it's God you can't get hurt), there's power in forgiveness, and our God is the God of the impossible.

HEALING IN THE MARKETPLACE

The second wave of this present move of God is about power to the streets, and we got to see that on the last night we were there. When one of the pastors came to get us we were standing around the hotel counter. He asked the hotel clerk, Christine, if he could have some aspirin for his headache. While she went to get some, Richard and I prayed for him and quickly all the pain left. She had a very puzzled look on her face when she returned and he told her he didn't need the aspirin anymore. Richard then began witnessing to her about the power of God to heal and save. She said she had a problem with her eyes and couldn't see far away. Richard said he felt sweat form on his body and realized a line had been drawn - either our God was going to back him up, or we were going to look foolish. Richard went for it and we began to pray for her eyes. After a minute we had her read something and kept putting it farther and farther away from her. When she said her eyes were much better, Richard asked her if she would like to accept Jesus into her heart and she said, "Yes, I think I would." It was so matter of fact! Richard led her in prayer and then invited her to come to church that night.

Now what's the chance that she would just happen to have the rest of the night off, that she would accept money from Richard for cab fare, that she would be able to talk her boyfriend into going to church, and that she would actually come? But she did! And of course, in God's economy, the church was packed that night beyond capacity and the only two seats left when she came were the two on the front row, vacated by Randy and Ben as they preached. So, there she was, front row and center when the power of God fell that night, and she witnessed it all. Richard said she had that "deer in the headlight look," but I didn't think it was that bad, and I remember answering a few questions for her about what was happening. Needless to say, she had quite an introduction to the presence of God.

We conducted 16 meetings in conjunction with 10 different churches in 3 cities on that trip. Conservatively, we saw 434 accept the Lord as their savior for the first time, 1,752 people who were backslidden return to the Lord, 353 people go through deliverance prayer, and 1,185 indicate they had received a physical healing. It was an incredible trip for many reasons. I got an anointing for receiving words of knowledge for healing by "feeling the pain" in my body – an anointing I had been wanting. We saw the raw power of God, seldom seen in the US, and we went into one of the most dangerous countries in the world and experienced the absolute "peace and protection" of God. Even now I would go back in a heartbeat, and have already done so on a few occasions.

CHAPTER 9

A MAJOR COMMITTMENT TO BRAZIL

We actually experienced what Randy often talked about in his teaching on "God Can Use 'Lil Ole Me" – that the healing ministry is a lot like "the thrill of victory, the agony of defeat." We went from great meetings in Colombia to meetings in Kentucky and Indiana in February, and then off to Argentina and Brazil in March. We went from thrilling to ok to totally thrilling. It's not that the meetings in the US weren't good, so much as we just didn't see nearly as much happen in US as we did down in Latin America, and the hunger was just not the same. The first night of five our night stay in Anderson, Indiana was a lesson for me, however, and has provided another story that I often tell.

I had gotten the anointing for words of knowledge by "feeling the pain" in Colombia, but now came the nagging suspicion: "Will it work here? Will the anointing last or was it just a one time thing?" On that first night, however, I got a word for arch pain that I felt in my right foot. I felt that fear come up once again, but I had determined not to let that stop me anymore, so I gave the word. Lo and behold, I saw one young woman stand when I gave the word. Later, that same young woman came to me and told me she had been healed from the pain when I gave the word. It turned out that she had an arch that flattened out too much, causing enflamed ligaments, and she also had bad bone structure that contributed to the problem. The doctors told her that she would have to live with the problem, since they couldn't guarantee that surgery would lessen the pain. She told me that when I gave the word and she stood, it felt like her arch was encased in a warm liquid and the arch was being "lifted up," as though she were wearing orthotics. She was pain free for the first time in many years! And the beauty of this was that this somewhat skeptical, too often overly analytical man got to watch her dance, run and jump during worship with absolute freedom over the next four days. It made an impression on me and I haven't held back since. I keep telling myself (and, later, anyone who'll listen in our meetings), "I may be wrong and look foolish, but what if I'm right and they get healed? It's worth any embarrassment."

LIFE-CHANGING MEETINGS, BUT SOME FUN TOO

We are doing something serious, something with life-changing results hanging in the balance. We are releasing people from captivity, perhaps healing years of pain, and speaking a prophetic word that releases destiny on a person. But don't ignore the fun!

We had one of those moments in this church. The worship team from Heritage Fellowship in Florence, KY, led by Dan McCollam, had come over to do worship. Now, there's just no other way to say it - we hadn't experienced much during the first four nights. On the last night, however, Dan got drunk in the Spirit, and he got the pastor drunk in the Spirit – for the first time! Now, Dan loves renewal, and there's just no other way to say it – he's a Holy Ghost drunk, and incredibly anointed. They were dying laughing as Randy gave words of knowledge. One of those words was for an itch on one side of the buttocks. No one responded to the word, so Randy gave it several times. Finally, Dan rose up and said, "Randy, it's not a word, it's your itch, so scratch it!" The place erupted in laughter - and there was breakthrough. It can't always be serious - we do have a fun God.

12 OF US TAKE ON ARGENTINA AND BRAZIL

In the first part of March, Randy, Ben and I, along with a team of 12 others, went to Cordoba, Argentina to minister in Omar Cabrerra

Jr's church. This is the trip that was supposed to happen the previous May, which I was to be on. We were to do 6 days of meetings in Argentina and then go to Brazil for the first time. It was exciting to be back in Argentina, and to see what this son of a legend was accomplishing on his own. After being with Omar Jr. for that time, it's easy to believe that one day we will hear many stories of the revivals he will lead in this country, and elsewhere.

Our team consisted of many anointed people. One couple was John and Mellie McKenzie from New York. John was about 76 at that time, and Mellie about 72. They had come to Randy a couple of years before and told him they wanted to learn as much as they could from his ministry, as they didn't have much time left and wanted to serve any way they could. They were particularly anointed for deliverance ministry and have been with Randy on several overseas trips. Rex, who would later become my replacement in November 1999, and his wife, Lois, were on the trip as well. There was Jerry Bryant, a Vineyard pastor from Nashville who was a longtime friend of Randy's. Although you might not have heard of this man, he moves with an anointing to "see" in the Spirit, much like Todd Bentley. Kirk Hinz, a CPA from Randy's church in St. Louis, was the only person who had been on one of Randy's previous trips to part of Argentina. I really appreciated his analytical, logical approach to things, and I loved seeing him get totally messed up by God. We also had Bill Johnson from Redding on the trip. Now, I have to be honest, I had not yet come to my complete admiration for this man when the trip began. I had been to his church for a conference back in the summer of 1997, while traveling with the worship leader from my church in San Diego, but he hadn't spoken so there was no way to know of the anointing that he carries. I did know that he and Randy had begun to build a strong bond, and that he credited Randy for increasing the healing anointing at his church in Redding when Randy had gone there in May, 1998. My impression of him was soon to change on this trip.

OMAR SR. WOULDN'T LET
IT RAIN ON THE MEETING

The meetings in Argentina were great, but one of the meetings that stuck out for me was a day meeting with about 128 pastors and leaders in a retreat area they own. The building was old and metal, with a concrete floor, but when it came to ministry time, they didn't care that there was no carpet to fall on. Randy taught on words of knowledge and only those who had never gotten a word were allowed to give them. Omar told us later that the ones getting the words were the lay leaders and those responding and being prayed for were the pastors – and he loved it. There was a lot of healing that day because of all the faith and hunger. Omar told us that many had ridden on a bus for up to 4 hours and would be going back home after the meeting.

That night we came back to the sports hall we had been doing meetings in; this time we were outside on the soccer field. And, of course, it was the one night when it threatened to rain. In fact, as I watched the black clouds moving towards us, I was sure that there was no way that this meeting wasn't going to be drenched.

We were hours away from Buenos Aires, but early in the meeting Omar Sr. called Omar Jr. and asked if it was raining yet. He hung up shortly thereafter, and it became clear he was interceding for this meeting. It soon became very apparent that the heavens had opened up all around us, but we were high and dry, even though the clouds were moving all around us. Omar, Sr. called during the meeting to make sure it still wasn't raining, and it never did.

After the message that night, Randy sent people to different areas of the field for healing, empowering, and repentance. There was a man there painting the stripes on the field to get it ready for the next day and you should have seen the look on his face when he looked up and saw about 350 people moving toward their respective lines. Toronto never had it so good.

TUMOR SHRINKS UNDER THEIR FINGERS

After these meetings, we went on the road to two cities where Omar had churches. From the first city, Villa Maria, there came a great story of healing. Randy and Kirk had gotten a word about ankle pain, and it turned out that a teenager had a bone growth on both feet that was causing a lot of pain. Bill Johnson and Ben prayed for him - Bill put his finger on one of the bone growths and Ben on the other. During the prayer, they both felt the growth just "disappear" under their fingers, and the teen reported that all the pain was gone!

In the city of Rosario, the team was insistent that Randy and Omar pray for them. Before the meeting everyone lined up in a field while both men went down the line. It was the first time that Randy had "officially" prayed for me since I had begun traveling with him. I know people thought this must happen all the time, but we were so busy, it just didn't.

THE BETTER THE STORY THE FASTER WE DROVE

The next day was to be a travel day going from Argentina to Brazil. We started out by driving back to Cordoba with most of the team in a van, and Randy, Bill Johnson, and myself in Omar, Jr.'s car. Although Omar likes to drive fast, Randy had already told him to try to keep it below 80 mph, because it scared him. Soon, though, Randy and Omar started swapping Holy Ghost stories, both having had some interesting experiences. The better the story, the faster Omar drove, whether he was telling it or listening to it. The only difference was that his hands would be flying all around, making gestures and rarely touching the steering wheel if he was telling the story. This unnerved Randy a little, but Bill and I were in the backseat, loving it.

We made it to Sao Paulo, Brazil and on Thursday morning we began the first meeting, one that was to lead to a fruitful relationship for Randy and the Brazilians.

THE NIGHT THE LIGHTS WENT OUT IN BRAZIL

If you will remember, this trip had come about because of the dramatic healing of a Brazilian pastor at the October, 1998 "Catch The Fire" Conference in Toronto. We were now meeting in the Foursquare Church headquarters church, pastored by Daniel Marins. That morning Randy spoke to the pastor's association, and about 1500 pastors and leaders were crammed into a church set up comfortably for about 1000. Somehow it worked, and it was a great way to whet their appetites, as 208 were healed from words of knowledge that 43 of them had gotten after Randy taught on this subject.

That night we came early to the church to pray for the sick, and the team got many words of knowledge which led to healing. After worship, Randy again went for words and another 229 got healed. When he went for salvation and for those who had backslidden, however, not much was happened – something felt wrong. One of the pastors came up to Randy and said that there were many pastors present whose churches weren't growing because of unconfessed sin. Randy felt a nudge of the Holy Spirit to go down this road, so he talked on holiness. His invitation for anyone to come forward who needed to confess and do business with God resulted in 85 pastors and leaders coming forward. It was an incredible time of repentance.

Then, at 10:15, it happened. The lights flickered a couple of times, and then went off altogether. In the pitch black, all over the building, people began worshipping and shouting praises to God. I thought, "When the lights come back on, this place is going to erupt." The lights never did come back on during the meeting, though. We did get a few flashlights on, enough to see by.

Now remember, many pastors and leaders had come forward to repent. They began coming up on the platform for Randy to lay hands on them and that started it. We just began wading through the crowd, laying hands on everyone we could get to. The lights were out in 8 states across Brazil and didn't come back on until after 1 AM, exactly the moment Randy and the team stepped out of the church. Hmmmmmmm! No one has ever been able to give an explanation as to why the power went out. All we knew was that we were having an effect. After one day and two meetings, 85 pastors and leaders had come forward for repentance and 468 people had been healed.

LIKE TOAST POPPING OUT OF A TOASTER

The next morning there was, as you might imagine, a high degree of expectation, Randy said he was going to preach that night on "Pressing In" and warned us that it might actually get scary - how true that was, for both the morning and evening session! That morning he taught on the biblical basis for healing. When he first started teaching that message, God had told him to have people stand up when they felt the healing anointing come on them. Randy was to bless them, and there would be healing. As Randy taught, the faith level was rising and it looked like toast popping out of a toaster, with people popping up all over the room. Then pandemonium broke out as almost everyone got to their feet shouting, jumping, and praising. The noise was deafening. We had never seen that level of passion and excitement – ever. This went on for 45 minutes. Randy didn't know what else to do, so he let the team go through the auditorium and bless them. There was no room and the seats were immovable, so we just climbed on them to get to those sitting in the middle of the rows. We started at 9 AM and it was 12:15 before Randy finally restored some semblance of order. He taught and ministered for another hour, and nobody left! We had 73 people indicate they had been healed during the teaching and when we prayed for those who still needed prayer, we had another 41 receive healing.

BILL WHO...? SOON EVERYONE WOULD KNOW

On Saturday morning it was decided that Randy and Ben would go out to the "gym" to check it out for the evening meeting. This was to be their big meeting and it was to be held in a gym, since the whole denomination had been invited to come. We kept wondering what kind of gym would hold the 10,000-15,000 people they said would be coming. That night we found that in the US, say in St. Louis, they would call it "The Arena" and in San Diego it would be the "San Diego Sports Arena." It was a huge doomed sports complex that could hold concerts, indoor soccer matches, or basketball games.

Bill Johnson spoke in the morning meeting while Randy was checking out the gym. This was to be my first realization of the anointing he carries. Bill spoke on "Pastoring the Renewal" and he basically told of he and his church's journey in pursuing the anointing of God for their community. He talked about how the surrounding community had thought of them as "that weird church up on the hill," and of how that had begun to change when an unbeliever got healed from cancer and started directing other people to the church, saying, "You need to get over to Bethel, they don't tolerate cancer."

He told a bunch of stories to encourage the Brazilian's hunger and faith, but it was one of our team who caused the stampede that morning. Kirk was sitting up on the platform with the rest of us when he suddenly moved to Bill's side at the pulpit. He told me later that the message was convicting him so much that he suddenly felt propelled up, like he couldn't **NOT** go up. Bill prayed for him for a moment and, when he fell out, the place erupted.

Even above the uproar of the congregation, Bill made one more point: "Everyone has as much of God as they want, there are no restrictions put on us. Elisha wanted a double portion, and this is a generation that has asked for the same thing - we have not asked for a normal revival." By this time, the Brazilian translator was shaking and had to hold onto the podium to stand. Everyone else was standing and shouting. Jerry Bryant shook out of his chair and Marcia, my translator, said that the jaw pain she had had for years had disappeared during Bill's message. When Bill touched the pastor of the church on the shoulder, he went down backwards, taking Bill with him. It was like an open invitation for everyone to start rushing the platform (surprise, surprise). We ministered for an hour, and the only reason we stopped was because Randy, who had arrived in time to see this pandemonium, had decided that we needed to add another session, to train on deliverance for the evening meeting. It was one of the most incredible meetings we had ever been in!

PASTOR'S WORDS SUM UP RANDY'S (AND OUR) MINISTRY

As incredible as that meeting was, it was just a prelude to the evening meeting, attended by twelve thousand plus. We walked in to find many worship teams and choirs on the floor of the gym, involved in incredible praise and worship with a decidedly Latin beat. It was a very festive atmosphere exalting the name of Jesus. Randy came on under a time crunch, having not gotten the platform until 30 minutes after they had let him know that many of the people had come from long distances by bus, and that he needed to move, since the city buses stopped running at midnight.

First, he went for words of knowledge for healing, and it was strong. The team got many words and within 25 minutes, when Randy took the last count, we had 1,073 people healed. We took many testimonies of healing, but the one that we all liked was this: a man came forward for prayer, walking with great difficulty, and Bill prayed for him. He had brain damage from a car wreck, couldn't move his arm and could barely walk. After a short time of prayer, he was moving his arm all around, walked with much more ease, and there was a lot of joy coming from him, which was endearing to us all.

Next, Randy gave a short, but powerful, message for salvation. He gave the call for all those who were backslidden or who had never given their lives to the Lord, and we were amazed at what happened – nothing! On a salvation call like this, Randy normally counts down from 10. By the time he got to 1, there was only one person who had come forward out of 12,000! He told me later he had all kinds of thoughts going through his mind – Did I blow it? Did they not understand? Could they not hear it? Still, he didn't stop. He listened to God and waited. I think there's probably a key there! He came against any spirits that would blind their minds to the gospel of Jesus, and it began to break. Soon, there were 300+ people up front, 25 of whom were accepting Jesus for the first time! It had been a spiritual battle, but God prevailed once more.

We concluded the evening by having everyone who needed healing go to one side of the gym floor, and everyone else who wanted a fresh touch from God to go to the other side of the floor. The team prayed for healing and the Brazilian pastors prayed for the refreshing. Ministry went from 11pm to 1:30am, and there were some incredible testimonies. Jerry dealt with a man who had a spirit of violence from martial arts. He came in violent and left like a lamb. Bill prayed for a man who was to have his foot amputated in 2 days. After prayer, he could walk with ease and without pain. He felt that he was healed and was going to get checked again before surgery. I checked in periodically as Randy prayed for a young woman who was legally blind. She couldn't see up close, and she certainly couldn't see the banner across the room. By the time Randy finished praying, she could read the banner and distinguish the colors.

We retired to the hospitality room, tired but overjoyed at what we had witnessed that day. It was then that Pastor Marins addressed Randy and the team members who had come at their own expense to be a part of this. He said, "You can't imagine how you've blessed us. One of the things of your ministry is love to the sinner. Much compassion. Normally when missionary or speaker comes, they are the last to arrive and the first to leave. You were the last to leave the gym tonight. This is meaningful because normally I'm the last to leave; the care and attention you've given is great. Pastors don't waste time with sheep in Brazil. You're not wasting time, but the

Holy Spirit is coming through you." That's just about the best endorsement you could hear about a ministry, huh?

ONLY WHAT GOD GIVES YOU
NOTHING MORE, NOTHING LESS

The final leg of this 19 day trip was in Belo Horizonte, at a Baptist Church. When the Brazilian contingent had spoken to him in Toronto the previous October, Randy was particularly taken with the Baptist pastor and wanted to accept his invitation to visit. We arrived very tired and, thankfully, they had purposely arranged it so that we had a night off. They took us out to a retreat area they owned, which had a swimming pool and volleyball courts. They prepared a delicious barbeque for us, and we got the chance to go out to a hill with a view of the city below and have a tremendous prayer time.

The meetings began on Tuesday night and the first thing that Randy did was to build trust with the people. They had not been exposed to the renewal like many churches we had been in thus far, and he didn't want them to focus on the manifestations, but on the power of God. He emphasized that we weren't looking for phenomena but for changed lives, and that the gifts of the Spirit are not for us but for others. That being said, he then went for words of knowledge for healing.

Bill Johnson had gotten a word for pain and pressure in the back of the left eye and he added he thought it was caused by sinus problems. God hadn't given him that, however – he had interpreted it that way. During the testimonies, a woman said she had come that night with pressure behind her eyes, but had been caused by the crossed eyes she had for 30 years. God healed her anyway - she had constant pressure and pain behind her eyes but as Randy prayed, the pain and pressure slowly got less and less, until it was completely gone and her eyes were straight!

I had a word for the right ear, but I didn't think it was about a hearing loss but an infection. It turned out that a young man had been kicked in the ear 5 years ago, it had become infected, and he had suffered a hearing loss. That night all the hearing came back. Bill and I were proving Paul right – we only know in part.

The next night showed us something else that has now become almost an automatic byproduct of going on one of these trips with Randy. Jerry Bryant was still with us, and he had a picture of a woman with nerve damage between the finger and thumb. A woman responded who matched the picture and had exactly what he had seen. She had not been able to open and close that finger and thumb, but complete mobility came back to her after prayer. Jerry said he had begun to move in much greater accuracy in prophesy and words of knowledge since coming on this trip. That's the testimony we hear from almost everyone who goes on one of these trips – their anointing goes up!

ANOINTING IS TRANSFERRABLE

The next day we moved to a Foursquare Church where we held a meeting for pastors and leaders, with about 1,200 attending that morning. Randy taught on recognizing words of knowledge for healing. 55 people came up after getting a word for the first time, and someone responded to every word. As Randy prayed over the group, there were 59 who indicated they were at least 80% better. To show it wasn't him but God who was in charge, he had the Foursquare pastor pray for the anointing to sweep across the room. The style was definitely different, the language was different, and the *volume* was completely different, but the results were the same. Another 53 indicated they were healed. To prove it crossed denominational lines, Randy had the Baptist pastor pray and another 15 were healed.

We actually thought the meeting was going to end then, but Randy was told that many of these pastors couldn't come back in the evening and Randy wanted to pray impartation for them. The Four-square pastor took the microphone, and all of a sudden everyone started pressing forward and yelling. They were hungry for prayer, crowding to the front so that there was hardly any room. Randy waded into the crowd while Ben and I looked on from the platform. At one point he looked back at us and mouthed, "Coward." He was right. There he was, completely engulfed by these pastors, pulling on him from every direction - it did look dangerous! But when he came up for a breather a couple of minutes later, we all dove in. As was typical on many of these trips, we had a short time for a quick meal and a little rest, and then it was time to be back for the 7:30pm meeting, to be held at the same church.

PRAYED FOR TERMINALLY ILL DURING MESSAGE

Twenty nine hundred people had jammed into this church and they had turned away at least another 1,000. It was hot, and it was crowded, but there was hunger. After Randy opened with words of knowledge and 235 were healed, he did something he had not done before. He called up everyone who had a terminal disease or who had something missing, and the team, which had dwindled down to six, would pray for them while he preached. I first prayed for a woman who had had several surgeries for a damaged retina in her right eye. She couldn't make out my features, even as close as I was to her, and she certainly couldn't make out the flower arrangement fifteen feet away on the platform. After soaking her in prayer and checking in with her, she could see my features clearly and could describe all the colors in the flower arrangement! Rex got to pray for a man whose voice box had been destroyed by cancer two years before. He literally couldn't make a sound and was in a lot of pain. After prayer, both Rex and I heard him speaking with a gravelly voice. We couldn't understand his Portuguese, but what a wonderful sound it was to him and to us!

LIVES TRANSFORMED

As I've said before, one of the biggest treats of those trips was seeing the lives of those around us get radically changed. I had a translator named Helga with me most of the time. She spoke 6 foreign languages and had always dreamed of traveling the world for CNN and speaking about Jesus while she worked. Many of her friends had told her she was crazy, but now this dream had been revived. She had been filled anew with God's power and I saw her begin to move in a different passion and anointing over the course of the four days we were there. I got an email from her about a year later informing me that she was in Italy, beginning to put her dream into practice. I also got to see the effect of this ministry on another young woman's life. She had come in lukewarm on the first night, but God had drawn me to her to pray for her and I "read her mail." She left the meetings with a new fire but, maybe more importantly, she had developed a relationship with a fellow Christian (me) that was to be very important to her several years later when she was desperate and in need of counseling and support. She came to the US, had a problem develop, and when she called I was able to have my wife, Carol, minister to her over the phone. Carol was exactly the person she needed at that moment, and I know God had arranged the whole thing.

Another woman we met down there in these meetings was Silvia. A psychologist, she is married to a successful businessman and spoke English very well, so she became very vital to all of us. She had never seen the power of God move as it did in these meetings, so later she began emailing me with questions. We later learned she had given up her practice, because she had seen the power of God and knew she couldn't get the same results through psychology. All she wanted to do now was pray for people, especially cancer patients in the hospital. God opened many doors for her to pray for people. Her hunger for the healing anointing led her to go to many healing conferences, and because she speaks English and carries the anointing, she has been very useful to Randy's team when they visit Brazil. We knew immediately about these people being touched by the meetings, but there were two stories we didn't hear about until later - one by email 6 months later and the others two years later when Randy went back to Belo.

THE "POINTING" ANOINTING BEGINS

During the last meeting at the Baptist church, I went up to the platform to look over the group just as we had gone into ministry time. As I looked over the group of approximately 600 women, I was drawn to one particular woman as if she were being spotlighted by a large beam of light. I knew absolutely nothing about her - I don't even know that I had even seen her before in the meetings. But I knew God was getting ready to do something. She was standing about 100 feet away, next to Silvia. As I got Silvia's attention, I motioned for her to be ready to catch the woman. I somehow knew she was about to turn and our eyes would lock. That's exactly what happened and, when it did, without saying a word, I just pointed at her - down she went, right into Silvia's arms.

This is what Silvia told me by email about 6 months later: The woman had been the most oppressed, depressed woman in the church. She was a total victim, on heavy doses of medication for depression and seemed to be in a hopeless place. She had received plenty of prayer but nothing seemed to make any difference. No one wanted to be around her, and God seemed to be very distant from her. When I prayed for her, Silvia said that the woman had gone down for a good 45 minutes. Several of the women who knew her were interested in seeing what would happen to her when she got up. Over the course of the next 6 months they had determined that she had become incredibly anointed and she was neither depressed nor oppressed any longer. She was a delight to be around and always had a sunny disposition. It was an amazing transformation. I've held onto this story because this is what I think we're going to come into. It's the one-step Jesus method — out of darkness and into His marvelous light. Freedom won't come with hours and hours of counseling or a ten-step method, but with the point of an anointed finger.

HE HAS NEVER BEEN THE SAME

This story didn't come to light until two years later. A man who was in the Baptist Church was in sin, and he felt as though God could never use him at the meetings. He could be a catcher, but that was about all – at least in his mind. One morning he awoke at 4 AM and smelled smoke. He got up to see if his house was on fire, and when he discovered that it wasn't, he went next door to see if the restaurant was up early cooking. They weren't. When he got back into bed, he saw smoke on his ceiling which was soon began descending toward him. He rolled over, but the weight began to push him into the pillow. Fearing he wouldn't be able to breathe, he moved his head to the side to get air, but end up pinned like that for two hours. When it finally lifted, he reached out to wake his wife, who began to shake violently when he touched her.

At the meeting, I had prayed and worked with him quite a bit. That night, I had motioned for him to come help translate for me but then gotten distracted and didn't see what had happened. As he began making his way toward me, stepping over bodies and steadying himself by putting his hand on people's shoulders, they began falling at his touch. People started reaching out to him to pray for them. He tried to decline saying, "No, I can't pray…" but it didn't do any good, and they continued to press into him, touching him and falling under the power. There had been a deposit in this man, a healing from sin, and a fire had been lit. When Randy and the team went back two years later he told the story, and how he had begun traveling, ministering, and leading the ministry team at his church.

Lives changed and transformed – that's what it's all about, and this 19 day trip had a lot of that. In the final analysis, on a conservative basis, we saw 860 salvations and rededications, and 3,828 people experienced physical healing. This trip to Brazil would be the first of many trips that Randy would take over the next eleven years to bring the fire of revival to this country. It had been prophesied that there would be another significant move of God coming through Randy's ministry, and many believe it's there in Brazil.

From Brazil it was time to head back to the US, but I was particularly excited about April's trips – Redding and San Diego!

CHAPTER 10

TOP TO BOTTOM IN CALIFORNIA

Randy had been to Redding for the first time the previous May; they were some of the most powerful meeting that he had ever experienced stateside. We were going to be there for nine days and there was great expectation, and for good reason - they turned out to be nothing like we had expected. Randy did a lot of new teaching during this time, and while the teaching and sharing from his heart was good, it was a hard week for him. Recognizing spiritual oppression, he decided to fast. He also made a statement I've never forgotten. He said, "The first time, we flew in under the radar, but this time the demons knew we were coming." That's what it felt like to him. It was also an unusual time, in that during the nine days we were there the shootout at Columbine High School in Colorado occurred.

As Randy and Ben taught during some of the morning sessions on deliverance, I wondered about something. We know from this deliverance teaching that we have the right and authority to call a demon into submission. We command that spirit to submit to the Lord Jesus and for the person to regain control of themselves. What would have happened if someone had been given this training and they would have had the presence of mind and boldness to say to the Columbine killers, "In the name of Jesus, I command that spirit of rage, anger, and murder to submit." I have heard stories of other instances when something like this happened and the person came to their right mind and stopped the harmful action they were about to commit. Just a thought.

HEALING IN THE MARKETPLACE

On my trip up to Redding to join Randy, something happened that has given me the opportunity to teach about two important things – what to do when you receive words of knowledge, and how the fear of man can stop what the Lord intends. I flew from San Diego to San Francisco, and then got on a shuttle bus to change terminals to catch the next plane to Redding. When the man sat on the bus directly across from me, I heard very plainly in my Spirit, "He was a football player and he has a hurt knee." I knew, without a doubt, that it was a word from the Lord, but I was paralyzed. So, I did what many of you might do – I started bargaining with the Lord. I told the Lord, "If he goes to my gate and sits off to the side, I'll go to him." Well, he went to my gate and ended up sitting as far off to the side. I argued with myself about how I would approach him and what I would say –I was still paralyzed. On the plane ride I bargained again. "Ok, if our eyes meet when we get to the terminal in Redding, I'll say something." He got off the plane, got his bag, got his rental car, and walked out of the terminal. Our eyes never met. Opportunity passed! I felt awful; I knew I had blown it. I repented to the Lord and asked for another chance. Guess what — He's the God of many chances!

Several days later, four of us went to a restaurant for lunch after the morning session. After a while the waitress came running up, apologizing, "I'm sorry it took me so long to get to you, I have a terrible headache and I took a pill and it's made me a little fuzzy." Someone at the table said, "Well, how's your headache now?" She said the pill hadn't helped, that she still had a pounding headache, but she had to be at work. Without thinking, I found these words tumbling out of my mouth and there was nothing I could do to get them back. "Well, we're Christians and we believe Jesus still heals and we'd love to pray for you." Huh? That's not like me. I want to be more like that, but that's not been my norm. Maybe it was being in the Redding atmosphere, where that sort of thing happens a lot - particularly through the ministry school they have.

Well, now the line in the sand had been drawn. There's not been an hour of great worship, no preaching of the word, and we're not in the anointing of the church. Will she respond and will it work here? After what seemed like several minutes of silence (probably no more than 10 seconds) she agreed to let us pray for her.

When I retell this story I now say, "So, I did what any good Pentecostal/charismatic person would have done. I smashed my hand into her forehead and shouted **BE HEALED IN THE NAME OF JESUS**!

You know, that model works and, if it's anointed, I'll take it anytime. But I don't think that model works well in a crowded restaurant. Instead, I gently touched her hand while the person on the other side touched her other hand. I prayed quietly, "Lord, I pray your blessing on Becky," (not a word of knowledge, she had a nametag on, but that would have been cool, huh?), "and in the name of Jesus I command all the blood vessels in her head to be at peace, for all the pain to leave, and for your peace to extend to all parts of her body. I command this headache pain to leave and not to return, and for her to be at complete peace, in the name of Jesus." It was literally a 30 second prayer.

Now the moment of truth - "How's your headache now?" She started moving her eyes all around, trying to "feel" the headache, but a big smile came on her face. She said, "There's no pain." We told her who we were, about the meetings at the church and invited her to come. Now, we should have asked her if she had a relationship with Jesus, who had just healed her, but for me, this was baby steps (remember the movie "What About Bob?") and this was all I could handle for the moment. I walked out of there thinking, "Yes! This is what it's all about." I was so thankful for a second chance. He's the God of second chances, and many more chances beyond, if we will but ask.

"HE DIED, WENT TO HEAVEN, AND CAME BACK." WHAT?

Another defining moment for us was the following. In one of the morning meetings, Bill was talking about how great the worship had been, and how we're going to be worshipping in heaven for eternity. Then he said casually, "We had a man die recently. He went to heaven, but he was sent back. He said heaven is a noisy place - he heard the prayers and praises of the Saints." Then Bill moved on, introducing Randy continued. I was sitting off to the side writing my report from the previous night's meeting, but I was suddenly at full attention. We talked later and both Randy and I had thought the same thing – Bill had just casually run through it, but he had just announced that a man had died, gone to heaven and come back. I wanted to know more about that, so we made arrangements to interview Don, the man who died and came back, on video. Since Randy was busy, I got to conduct the interview.

In February, Don had learned that he had pancreatic cancer. It was risky surgery, but he found a competent doctor he trusted, and they scheduled the surgery in early March. The church and the intercessors prayed for two weeks before the surgery. He came through the operation with flying colors, but crashed the next day with internal bleeding. He said he died, left his body, and found himself face to face with Jesus. Jesus wrapped his arms around him and covered him in the blood. He came back to his body, but spent next six days in critical condition. His body swelled up, and they had to do more surgery, but couldn't give him anesthesia. His wife was by him, constantly praying that there would be no pain.

Remarkably, he remembered nothing of this, and felt never any pain. During this time, his grown, newly born-again son would come into the room. He saw an angel standing in the corner of the room, looking intently at Don lying in the bed. After some time has passed, the angel made a motion, as though he had been holding a large bowl and now it was spilling over into Don. Was this perhaps the prayers of the saints, as described in Revelation 5? When he finally came around, the first thing he asked was, "Who turned the radio off?" He had been bathed in the prayer and the praises of the saints and he described the sound of worship as gloriously full. Not deafeningly loud, but full. As he told me this incredible story, you should have seen his face. He beamed, sharing his story with anyone and everyone. He especially likes to talk about how important prayers are and the magnificence of the worship of Heaven..

THE HEALING ANOINTING JUST GOES HIGHER

There were so many things that happened on this trip, and so many healings - I'll give just a few. Early in the week a woman had come to the meetings and responded to a word of knowledge for breathing problems due to smoking. It wasn't easy for her - she even had to go through a panic attack to go smoke - but she walked out of the meeting with absolutely no desire to smoke. She came back a few nights later with a friend who was desperate. This friend didn't feel good, had driven over two hours to get there, and wasn't used to these kinds of meetings – but she was desperate all the same.

During the pre-service prayer time she got a taste of what God wanted to do that night as she was touched by God's love. She went forward during the altar call to re-dedicate herself to the Lord, and then responded to a word of knowledge for healing. Bill Johnson and a prayer team member prayed for her scoliosis and I prayed for her sore knee. Her knee got healed quickly, so I moved on, but I checked back with her later. The prayer team member had continued to "soak" her in prayer, as the twisting of her spine straightened out and all the pain left. It was just her night, as God poured out His love, deliverance, and healing on her. I witnessed gold dust all over her, and while she was on the floor, Bill and the prayer team member saw a small feather float down and land in her hair. I think it was a sign to her (and us) of His presence. In the end, she just got gloriously blessed with laughter and left the meeting a different woman!

The next night was once again semi-organized chaos. It was 11 PM, people were leaving, and I was reading off words of knowledge for healing and directing people to the back of the room for prayer. God is always able to make something out of this chaos, though. A young woman named Kim was sitting close by on the steps when I called out "sores in the mouth." She suddenly realized that the three sores in her mouth that had caused her such pain, were gone!

Sheryl had a total transformation and literally changed before our eyes. She had been in excruciating pain for the past 25 years. She had been through six surgeries and now had a steel rod in her back. Her back was twisted, causing her left leg to be shorter and turned outward - she couldn't stand or walk without limping. During prayer, the twisted spine returned to normal and the pain left. Her leg grew out and straightened. I checked in with her faithful friends and the prayer team members who had been with her all evening, and I got to witness this work in progress. By the end of the evening, she was literally glowing. Best of all she had rededicated her life to the Lord! These were just glorious meetings, although not like what we had expected going in.

"AMERICA'S FINEST CITY" BECOMES "AMERICA'S ANOINTED CITY."

Of course, I had told Randy many times about the Vineyard church we attended and about what God was starting to do in San Diego, which was to be the second leg of this "California tour." Now, normally, the senior pastor of the church needed to issue the invitation and the event would be coordinated with other churches in the city, so as to ensure the ability to reach as many people as possible. I knew it was because of our connection that he decided to come to San Diego without following his usual procedures. To this day, I still believe that he was the forerunner of what God was setting up for us in San Diego and what He wanted to do with the churches of the city.

In late April, Randy visited a church on the old Naval Training Center. The Navy had turned the property over to the city and, while the city was deciding what to do in terms of developing it, they had rented out some of the buildings to various tenants. One of these tenants was a church, occupying this 24,000 square foot building that they believed was to be used as a revival center for San Diego. In May, they planned a week of meetings with Marcos Witt, Tommy Tenny, and Wes Campbell. Then, in September, they had scheduled Carlos Annacondia for 9 days of outdoor crusades. It was a time of many churches coming together to war for the harvest of the city and to strengthen the churches in the area. As was often the custom with Randy's meetings, his office had recommended that one of his Resource Teams come in prior to the meetings to train a ministry team, so Bill and Barbara Cassada had come in just a few weeks before. That was a major key to our ministry, as many of the pastors saw the value of having their people trained in healing and deliverance.

The first meeting was on a Wednesday night, and there were about 700+ in attendance, from many different streams. About 95% raised their hands when Randy asked if who had never heard him preach. He was going to give his testimony, but mostly he just rambled. It was a good rambling, though - afterwards, many of our friends came up to us and told us that they had seen his humble heart and they understood why we were traveling with him.

By the third night, many had been healed as words of knowledge for healing were given, many had been set free from demonic attack, and everyone was excited about a fresh anointing for "more" of God. One of the most dramatic healings was of a woman who had been ill with many afflictions for 25 years. An accident had left her with pins in her back, but the power of God touched her so profoundly that she could now do all sorts of deep bends and sit-ups – something that was impossible before the meeting. Her husband was absolutely speechless as he watched his wife receive healing!

These were important meetings to San Diego, and to Carol and I. It brought fresh credibility to us and it led to our teaching in four churches during Randy's vacation time over the summer. That was invaluable time, establishing us in ministry, as you will see in subsequent chapters.

CHAPTER 11

FAVORITE PLACES
KOREA, FLORIDA AND NEW MEXICO

This was my third trip to Korea, but it was to be definitely different from the first two. That was evident right from the beginning, as we landed in Seoul and were taken to the Ritz-Carlton. It was as nice as you might expect. While we enjoyed it, Randy was not really comfortable with how "nice" it really was. He's more of a "down-home" kind of guy who doesn't have to stay in a fancy place to be happy. They also insisted in getting him his own room, so Ben and I stayed together. Ben and I felt for Randy at other times too. When we would go for a meal with our hosts, Randy would be with them and many times they would be talking in Korean. At least we had each other, but Randy had no one. Such is the price when you're the "big cheese," as we told him.

After resting that first day, we began the meetings by having Randy and Ben go to an independent church on Sunday morning, while I and our Korean host, Sam, went to a smaller independent church. In my previous trips to Korea, I had been used to staying in someone's home and doing smaller meetings like this. This group was hungry and the meeting was really fun. It also gave me a story that we have used in our training – although not with a happy ending. I was asked to pray for a man with back pain. After praying for a little bit, I felt like the Lord told me it was because of unforgiveness. When I asked him if he had unforgiveness toward someone, he indicated it was his father. I explained to him the importance of forgiving, but no amount of talking or reasoning would move him from his position. Even when I offered to pray for the Holy Spirit to "help" him be willing to forgive, he wouldn't budge. He was not ready to forgive. I blessed him, prayed for the Holy Spirit to help him to forgive, explained all this to his pastor, and walked away without him being healed.

IT WORKS FOR ME, TOO

Afterwards, Sam and I went to join Randy and Ben at the other meeting, where I got to teach on the healing model and words of knowledge for healing. This was the first time that Randy had used me to teach – I was nervous and excited at the same time. You know, it didn't even faze me when only one person came up to say they had a word of knowledge after I finished teaching. I just remembered the time I had seen Randy teach to 1,000 people in Argentina and only 6 came forward. I said the same thing – "if you think you *might* have gotten a word, would you be willing to risk and step out so that someone could get healed?" The same thing happened in this group as did then - 20 streamed forward out of this group of 200. The words were accurate and many got healed. Amazing. It works here, too, and it works when *I* teach it!

RANDY ACTUALLY GOT MAD

Next, we moved to a large Methodist Church in Inchon. During one of the sessions, Randy taught on "A Biblical Basis for Healing." We wondered if the message would transfer to here, so we were glad to see about 34 people stand, and 23 come forward at the end of the message to give testimonies about how God had healed them during the teaching. Amazing!

While on this trip to Korea, I saw Randy get angry for the first and only time. He had taught on recognizing words of knowledge for healing and many had come forward to give them for the first time. Some were pastors and leaders, but most were not. The Korean people have great reverence for their pastors, so many of the people started walking out of the meeting when they realized that "regular" people were giving the words. Randy pointed out to them that they were actually dishonoring the greatest "Mok-sa-neim" (phonetic spelling for honorable pastor), in the form of the Holy Spirit who was moving through these people. Hopefully, they got it.

At another point, we got to go to a Methodist church that was still in the process of building their building to hold 3,000, so we held the meeting in the basement, with about 1,000 people in attendance. It was a night for healing. Ben got to pray for a 5 year old little girl who had been deaf since birth and could only hear with the help of hearing aids. She was completely healed and gave her testimony before the church. One woman had disc pain for 18 years and another for 20 years. Both were healed and demonstrated how they could do things they had not been able to previously do without pain.

A WILD, SCARY RIDE ACROSS SEOUL

Randy had made a commitment to fly to Singapore to do some meetings for the weekend, so he left me, Ben, Sam and his family in Seoul, where we spoke at a Presbyterian Church. On my previous trips to Korea, and for most of this trip, there had been a lot of freedom in ministry time. Not so this weekend. Our host pastors informed us we had to be out of the school building they rented by 9:50pm, and I had only 15 minutes (in English) to speak. I was so excited and grateful about being in a position to speak and minister, and at the same time I was thinking to myself, "Help! Randy, you didn't tell me it would sometimes be like this!" God backed us up, though. There was tremendous power in that meeting, and we walked out of the building exactly at 9:50pm.

Randy came back the next night, just in time for the meeting in a small church of about 250, and Ben and I had the ride of our lives. We were being transferred to another hotel on the other side of Seoul. One of the men had been assigned to come and get us to the church. He obviously had been told to get us there on time. Now, 5 o'clock rush hour traffic in Seoul has got to be every bit as bad as Los Angeles or New York - maybe even worse. All I know is, it was the scariest ride Ben and I had ever taken. We were so glad to be at the church, and glad to have Randy back in control as the "big cheese." We were also glad to be in a meeting where the power of God was so evident and anything and everything could and was happening.

From there, we moved on to the last church on this trip for 2½ days of meetings. It was there that we learned a little about the Korean mindset, and also saw how God will go to any lengths to show that He will not be boxed in by man.

GOD MAKES HIS POINT – DRAMATICALLY

During the meetings we were all drawn to a man in a wheelchair. He had been paralyzed in an auto accident, and as we took turns praying for him, he started to get some movement back in his arms and legs. He became a key element as God made a statement to these Koreans. These people had definitely seemed hungry, but more to be blessed than to receive it and give it away. It wasn't until the last session, on the day we were to leave, that a woman pastor who spoke exceptionally good English was able to tell me that many times, in Korean churches, they fear the average lay person getting anointed, because he or she may leave and start a new church with some of their people. It makes for a "bless me club" atmosphere, doesn't it? God had something to say about all this, and He always has the last word, doesn't He?

Randy taught on the healing model and then asked how many needed healing in their bodies, and at least 75 % raised their hands. Then he surprised them. He told them they were to pair up and pray for each other. They were the prayer team – not he, Ben or I. Very hesitantly they began to do this and we began to get the testimonies. We know of at least 33 who were healed, and then the miraculous happened. Looking back on it, we now see God's hand in this.

We had originally been scheduled to leave at 3:00pm, but had changed it to a later flight. We began the meeting at 10:30am and would have had to end the meeting at 12:30pm if we had not changed the flight. It was at 1:15pm that we began to hear the gasps and clapping and cheering as we were taking testimonies. Suddenly, everyone was clearing a way, as the man, once in the wheelchair, began walking toward the platform to give his testimony. He told his pastor and everyone else he had felt heat go up and down his spine and now he could walk. The man who had prayed for him? A 32 year old man who had never prayed for anyone in his life! God could not have emphasized more dramatically that He wants to use **all** of us. The only qualification is, "All authority in Heaven…and lo, I am with you always."

Later, as I wrote the report of the meetings, I said that we ended up being delayed two and a half hours past the time that we were supposed to leave, and Randy and Ben only had an hour and a half window to catch the last plane out of LA to St. Louis. We always emphasize that there is a cost to this ministry, that while everyone else is off to Sunday brunch, you may still be in church praying for someone if you're on the ministry team. As it turns out, they didn't make it home until the next day, but God showed up big time and it wouldn't have happened if we had taken the earlier flight.

A "CREDIBLE WITNESS" GETS US INTO JACKSONVILLE

In June, it was first off to Jacksonville, Florida, and then to Albuquerque. The meetings in Jacksonville came about through the relationship this independent Word of Faith Church had with the American leader in Colombia, Randy McMillin. Those meetings in January had been so significant that McMillin had told the pastor he should have Randy in. There was still some reluctance, but when Randy's office sent them a tape of Randy's teaching on "God Can

Use Little 'Ole Me," it sealed the deal. There is a testimony on one of the tapes of Randy Ostrander. Randy had been a well known athlete in Florida who went on to become a well-known Word of Faith pastor. He had severely hurt his neck, which three surgeries and lots of prayer had not helped, but at meetings in Melbourne, Florida in '95 he had been miraculously healed when Randy prayed for him. This church knew about Randy Ostrander; he was their "credible witness." So, even though Randy's laid-back style was different for this very alive Pentecostal church, the stage was set for some monumental meetings, and some dramatic healings.

There are several things that stick out in my memory about these meetings. I remember one of the elders, Keith, telling the story of how he couldn't be at the first night's meeting because of work. But he was listening to the service on the radio, when Randy called out a word of knowledge for sacroiliac pain. As soon as the word was given, all his pain left! That afternoon, Ben had asked God to give him some very specific words of knowledge, and for a short time, he went deaf. Now, that's a specific word of knowledge by "feeling" the condition in your body! When Ben gave that word that night in the meeting, two people responded and received their hearing back! We had a young man named Bruce from Randy's church in St. Louis traveling with us for this trip. As he began praying for a woman in a wheelchair she wanted to try to stand. A gift of faith came upon him and he helped her up. He held her hands as she gingerly began to take very cautious steps. Then more and more. Soon, amid the cheers and gasps of the surrounding people, she was walking under her own power. One man who knew her said she couldn't take more than two steps before. And the look on Bruce's face was priceless. It's that look that says, "God, I don't believe this, and I'm soooo glad you let me be a part of it."

The next night, Randy did his message on "Pressing In." This is a message about being desperate for God. Often times it had caused the congregation to rush Randy for him to pray for them - before he even finished his message! It had not, however, happened the last three times he had given the message, so we were wondering what would happen this night. At one point a woman approached him on the platform – a hungry, desperate woman who was not afraid to risk embarrassment. We were very aware that the most desperate people at that time were often the Koreans, and this woman was, in fact, Korean.

Anyway, this act caused several of the ushers to get a little nervous. They were not used to this, and I could tell that the head usher I was sitting next to didn't like it that his guys allowed that woman to get to the speaker. The usher who was sitting on the other side of me began to shake and I put my hand on him and said, "More, Lord," as he fell between the rows of chairs. He soon crawled out to the aisle. I thought he was just looking for more room to lie down, but soon he was up and running toward Randy, who gave him with a gentle touch. Now, the ushers were even more nervous.

When the pastor's wife couldn't stand it anymore and rushed the platform, all heaven broke loose. Randy was immediately surrounded by people reaching for him, seek an impartation. We prayed for everyone. Then, at about 11 PM, we shifted the emphasis to healing, and we saw a dramatic one.

A woman named Vickie had strep B, complicated by lupus, and had come in tremendous pain that night. She had had the condition for the past year and a half. The doctors had given up on her, saying she was terminal and there was no cure. But God had told her three different times to get prayed for by Randy. After only a few minutes of prayer, the power of God hit her. All her pain left, and she later testified that she felt completely different. The friends she had come with said she looked like a different woman. What incredible meetings and what a great church!

ALBUQUERQUE
OUR FIRST SPEAKING INVITATION

Next, it was on to Albuquerque for a God at War Conference with Randy and Dr. Gregory Boyd. These meetings were memorable for many reasons, but I'll just focus on two. Bill and Barbara Cassada, who had traveled with Randy prior to me, had done the ministry team training here a month earlier and had come back for this conference. They had spoken in a Foursquare church the night before Randy's meetings began, and Randy had them share on the first night what had happened in that meeting.

While there was a great sense of "the party" at this particular church, Bill had sensed God telling them to bring a message about His Holiness. They both preached, but God used Barbara's gesture to make a point. The church wants to see His Glory, but there has to be purity. She had just talked about Ananias and Sapphira and to emphasize the point she had pointed her finger. All during the message there had been a couple squirming under conviction. At the exact moment she pointed her finger upward, the light fixture above this couple exploded, rained down on and burned them, even singeing the woman's slacks. When the call for ministry was given, they were the first to run to the altar, where she re-dedicated her life to purity and he got saved.

The other memorable thing about these meetings was that it was the first time that Carol, who had accompanied me for this part of the trip, and I were asked to speak at a local church after the meetings. Looking back on it now, I remember that I wasn't nervous and, in fact, felt very confident. I just had an attitude that I had been around Randy and his anointing so long that I expected God to show up when I said, "Come Holy Spirit." I don't think I had any illusions of grandeur that it would be the same as in Randy's meetings, but I expected Him to come – and He did! It also gave us practice in moving with the Spirit, as He gave Carol a completely different message during worship. The message was "Giants in the Land," regarding renewal, a message we still occasionally teach today. We prayed for the sick and they got healed, and when we had an altar call for those wanting a fresh touch, almost everyone came. A call for the youth, and they too came. We also had the opportunity to pray for many marriages, as we had told a little of the story of our marriage being healed, and many responded. We went back to San

Diego very excited about what God had done, and prepared for the meetings we had scheduled during an almost two month break before the next trip with Randy.

CHAPTER 12

OUR OWN MINISTRY BEGINS

The break in San Diego was pivotal in our ministry. Up until that time I hadn't really done much teaching or speaking while traveling with Randy. He was mentoring Ben, and I understood that. I had told him that my fondest desire was that one day I would be able to lead meetings, teach on healing, and move with the leading of the Holy Spirit. Since Randy had come to San Diego in April and had highlighted Carol and me, there was now some favor on us, and we were getting our chance. I honestly don't think I ever stopped to think, "What if He doesn't come when I say 'Come Holy Spirit,' like it would happen in Randy's meetings." In hindsight, I guess it should have been of some concern to me, but I just forged ahead believing that our meetings were going to be like Randy's or Bill and Barbara's.

We were first asked by a Vineyard church located in the eastern part of San Diego to come do the prayer ministry training. At that time, it was common for the resource team (Bill & Barbara) to do teaching on deliverance on Saturday morning and teaching on the 5 Step Healing Model and Words of Knowledge for Healing in the afternoon. Looking back now, I can't imagine how we did that. And what we now know is that there's no way we could do justice to either subject with so little time. These days we try to devote an entire weekend to either healing or deliverance.

Nonetheless, there we were for our first teaching that Saturday morning. What was amazing was that everything we had been seeing in Randy's meetings as he or Ben taught on deliverance and then called out the spirits that had been harassing people, happened in this meeting. People manifested, people who had never ministered in this way before started to manifest, and people got set free. When we taught on words of knowledge, most acknowledged they had not moved in this gift before, but 8 people gave 11 words and someone responded to every one of them. Many people were healed that day. When we went for a time of impartation, the Spirit fell and many were touched as we prayed for them, or even just pointed at them. What had started in Brazil in March was still there, even in San Diego! Two young women got the laughter, so we just brought many people over to them. As these women touched them, the people would fall out. You should have seen the looks on the two young women's face - they may never have been the same after that. We often wonder about what God does with people after meetings like this. I know there have been defining moments in conferences or meetings, when something was different in the anointing I walked in.

I certainly wouldn't want to take all the credit for what happened to one couple, because I know they were hungry and used by God before that meeting, but I do believe we had a hand in further fanning the flames of passion in them. They came under our teaching several more times in the next few years, and went on to oversee the Healing Rooms of San Diego, where their fire, passion and anointing is literally helping to transform the healing ministry in San Diego.

A PRACTICAL DEMONSTRATION

The next weekend we were once again doing the training on a Saturday, this time at an AG church. It was during this meeting that we started doing something that has been foundational to all our meetings – bringing someone up with pain to demonstrate how to pray for the sick, with either us or someone from the congregation doing the praying. I had actually seen this done in Francis and Judith MacNutt's meetings, and I thought it was a great way to demonstrate prayer by the "little ole me's."

In this meeting, I ended up praying for a woman who had pain from her hip all the way down to her foot. It became clear that I would have to come against an afflicting spirit because of the increased pain she experienced as I prayed. As I did, she rested in the Spirit and I had Carol and her prayer partner "soak" this woman. Every once in a while I would check in on her and she could only mumble something like, "Great, the Spirit is so heavy on me." After doing the teaching and exercise on Words of Knowledge, we prayed for everyone who still had pain or sickness, and many got healed as Carol prayed for them. It's interesting that Carol generally recognizes that she is anointed and used by God for deliverance and deep inner healing, when the enemy seems to have an easier time of coming in and robbing her of the fact that she is also powerfully used for physical healing. As I remind her of some of these stories from past meetings, she has to acknowledge that they happened, but if you were to ask her about physical healings, she would tell you she isn't used very much for that.

IMPARTATION HAS BECAME
A HALLMARK OF OUR MINISTRY

Our next meeting was in a Foursquare church, located in the eastern part of San Diego. It was during this week that we started to understand what the warfare surrounding this ministry would be like. The week before, we had experienced a lot of warfare prior to the meeting. This time we experienced the attack on each of us during the meeting. I had felt the Lord saying to me, and it was confirmed by Carol independently of me, that there was going to be some special and deep impartation during the ministry time. That turned out to be very prophetic and true. Both of us felt heavy and sluggish during our teaching and when we compared notes during lunch, Carol talked about how scattered she had felt. Several people assured her that her teaching had been very good, and I tried to confirm that, since I knew exactly what she was to teach. It's interesting how the enemy was trying to undermine our thinking and confidence. God wanted to do something very special, and the enemy didn't want that to happen.

God was pushing me to exercise my faith on this day as well. When we teach on recognizing words of knowledge for healing, we often say "Faith is spelled R-I-S-K." Many times I have to emphasize, "If you *think* you *might* have gotten a word, step out and come forward and give it." Earlier I felt like I had heard the Lord say, "During your teaching I'm going to heal, so have them stand up when they feel the healing anointing on them, and then bless them." This is something Randy did often when he taught "A Biblical Basis Of Healing," and I also remember reading Bill Cassada's report about hearing God tell him to do this while he was traveling with Randy the first time. That's fine for them, but it's scary when it's you! I did it, though, and was amazed by the results. During my teaching that afternoon, four people stood up and I blessed them. I talked to one lady afterwards who, when I blessed her, felt all the pain in the area around her heart lift off of her! In fact, there was a lot of healing that afternoon at that meeting when Carol and I prayed, and when the members of the congregation prayed.

Here's another instance of the "little ole me" principle at work. Gail was one of those at the training. She was the church secretary and was a member of the prayer team, but hadn't prayed for anyone. At the end of the afternoon, we prayed for impartation before leaving. She had rested on the floor and was now starting to rise up. I often kid when I say, "It must have been a spirit of ornery on me, but I just waved my hand at her and said 'take more.'" With that, she was back on the floor. She told us later that she felt something come upon her. Then when she went home to check on her husband who was not feeling well, she found him passed out on the floor with a high fever. She rushed him to the emergency room. When the doctor got them into the examining room, she noticed the Prayer Ministry badge on Gail. She said, "If you believe in prayer, you should pray because his fever is quite high and I'm concerned about him."

Immediately, oil formed on Gail's hands and she laid hands on her husband, praying. Within a minute, all the fever was gone and he was asking why he was there. Someone in the next stall, which was separated only by a curtain, heard this and came to Gail to ask if she could come pray for their uncle. He was dying of cancer and had already had his legs amputated at the knees - they didn't expect him to live through the night. We don't know what happened to the man, other than he flew home to his state two days later.

By now, a chain reaction had started. The word was getting around. All told, 20 people sought her out that night. She knows of at least 5 people who were significantly healed, and she led 5 to the Lord! She got there at 5:30 in the evening and didn't leave until 5 in the morning. She had never done this kind of thing before! When she went to church for the 9 AM service and told her pastor what had happened, he did something very smart - he had her pray for everyone who wanted that anointing. Wow! We tell her story a lot — she's one of our heroes - and it shows what God can do with a "little ole me."

CHAPTER 13

A HARD TRIP — PAIN AND NO SLEEP

My next trip with Randy was to Hungary and Austria. I have to say, it was the hardest trip for me physically. I developed cramp-like stomach pains, in addition to intense sleep deprivation during the week or so we were gone. Let me explain. For most of the trips, it had been Randy, Ben and I in a room. For these meetings, however, one in Gyor, Hungary and the other in Schladming, Austria, we had a small team accompany us. Charles and Anne Stock, pastors in Harrisburg, PA, had arranged this trip for Randy, and they were there with a couple from their church. Che Ahn, from Harvest Rock church in Pasadena, CA, was another of the speakers and he had a couple of people with him. Rex Burgher came along, as did Mike Ellis, a businessman from the Atlanta area. Mike had traveled with Randy in the beginning, just after Toronto, and he was starting to reconnect with Randy's ministry. Rex, Mike and I roomed together.

Now, I've got to tell you, I really do love these guys. They are wonderful, anointed men of God, full of integrity and passion for the Kingdom - but they snore! And I'm not talking about a little buzzing sound - I'm talking about "sounds like a bulldozer is coming into the room, rattle the walls" kind of snoring. So there I was, with stomach pain, cramps, and no sleep. I'm sure (actually, I know) I wasn't very pleasant on that trip. I think they've both forgiven me — I'm still working on my part, though (just kidding). The funny thing is, neither could hear the other, and they never woke each other up.

NOT THE PICTURE I EXPECTED

One of the things I tried to do while reporting on the meetings was to paint a picture of what God was doing around the world, what it looked like, and how the people responded. I also wanted to paint a picture of what the people looked like, what the environment was, and how God moved so the people could get a feel of what it was like in a foreign culture.

Now, I had a predetermined concept of what we would be seeing in Hungary. My wife's family came from Hungary, and my picture of that country had been developed from television scenes I had seen and my firsthand knowledge of "grandmother." I had a picture of older women, worn with time, large, dressed in dark clothes, with a shawl over their heads - this is how I had often seen the news footages of women from this area of the world. I couldn't have been more surprised when we entered into the school gym where the first conference was being held and found it filled with young, colorfully dressed young men and women, passionate in worship for Jesus, and hungry for more of God. We had great worship, long sustained moments of silence where you could almost hear the "hush of God in His holiness." Gold dust came on many - something completely new for them.

In Hungary, we got to do something that we didn't get to do the entire year that I had traveled with Randy - we went sightseeing. A couple graciously offered to take us into Budapest after Randy finished the Sunday morning service, so that afternoon off we went to see such sights as the castle high above Budapest. It was wonderful, but I also remember the ride back. It was late at night, in a van whose shocks seemed to be nonexistent, and I had stomach pains once again – not fun.

WILL AHNOLD BE THERE?

Next, it was off on a van ride to Schladming, Austria, to a mountain resort where they were holding a conference with Randy and Che as the speakers. It's a beautiful area, and we had been told it was Arnold Schwarzenegger's favorite resort. After receiving that knowledge, several of the team took to saying "It's not a tumor" or "I'll be back" anytime the opportunity presented itself (there's a rumor that I started that, but I'll deny it). I have several observations from these two meetings that I'll share.

In both Hungary and Austria, Mike Ellis would minister deliverance and inner healing for several hours to people while the speaker would be teaching and then into the ministry time and beyond. One time in Austria, I ministered to a young woman who was mad at God for the husband she had. When the power of God hit her, she developed a pain in her chest. Knowing this was going to be very deep, I called Mike over and he and some others ministered to her. She had come out of a Catholic background and had experienced a lot of sexual and physical abuse in her life; she had a lot of guilt about sex. Mike spent until 1 AM in the morning ministering to her the love of the Father. He did this time after time. It is the price he pays for the anointing he carries, but he loves it.

A DIFFERENT CULTURE

While doing the Austrian conference, we encountered a difference in culture that took some getting used to. The meetings were held in a large hall across from the main lodge. To get into the hall, you passed by the bar set up in the hotel. Now the Austrians weren't shy about visiting the bar on their way into the hall. They don't look at drinking the same way we do. It's as natural for them to have a beer with their meal as it is for us to have a coke.

Well, as an aside, Randy had a large team accompany him to Curitiba and Recife, Brazil in 2000. There were nine Austrians on that part of the trip. The first day, after the morning meeting, we were all at lunch, and the Austrians all had a beer. The pastor of the Brazilian church came to Randy and told him he knew about the custom, but his people would think these people weren't Christian if they saw them drinking. The Austrians, of course, agreed to comply with the pastor's request not to be seen drinking. When we got to the church in Recife, the largest Anglican church in Brazil, they hosted a dinner for us on the first night - tablecloths, waiters in tuxes and everything, including wine! What was a forbidden custom in the southern part of Brazil was perfectly okay in the northern coastal city. I was quickly instructed to go around and tell everyone that if they wanted to have a glass of wine it was ok there.

FINGER, GROW!

While in Austria, Che told this story. On a very busy Easter Sunday service that year at his church, a man had approached him during ministry time. He had just had a major portion of his finger cut off in a gardening accident caused by his young daughter. The doctor had not been able to reattach the finger and said he would have a stump for the rest of his life. He wanted Che to pray for him, but there it was, one of the busiest Sundays of the year. Che said he just quickly touched the bandaged finger and said, "I command this finger to grow out in the name of Jesus" and moved on. A few weeks later the man came back and showed him that the finger had grown back about 90% and was starting to grow a fingernail! Most importantly, his daughter, witnessing the power of God, had given her heart to Jesus and was now on fire for God! I have always remembered that story, especially when someone comes to me as we are walking out of the meeting and wants prayer - and it's never just a little thing. God's power, mercy, grace, and incredible love for us goes so much further than our wordy prayers. I know there are times when we need to persevere in prayer, but there's also times when a two word prayer is dynamite in the hands of an awesome God.

RANDY GETS SET UP

Randy got set up by God. On the last morning, he was teaching on the principles of healing. In doing this, he tells a story of praying for the lengthening of a person's leg and how he really didn't have any faith for it. When he says this, he usually adds that he actually hates doing this. It comes out of seeing so many charismatic people pray for the lengthening of legs while he was still a Baptist pastor and he thought it was hokey.

Just as he was saying these exact words, a man approached him. Now, Randy was used to being interrupted during his "Pressing In" message, but never during this one. He came right up to Randy and told him he had one leg shorter than the other one and was constantly in pain. The man had such a look of faith on his face that Randy stopped teaching and started praying for his leg to grow. It was a good inch shorter and was confirmed by two chiropractors who were on the team.

By now, many people were coming up to see what was happening. Randy continued to talk about what he was doing, which provided a great clinic on praying for the sick. Interestingly, Randy had gotten a sharp pain in his leg while speaking but had thought he would just give it at the end of the message. It was actually for this man, though, and for what would happen next. As this man got healed from constant pain for 15 years, Randy knew he wasn't to continue teaching, but to stop and pray for anyone with a shorter leg or with hip problems. We had sixty-five people answer that call and we ministered for the next hour. Many, many people got healed — all because a man was desperate for his healing, and because Randy was obedient to what he heard God say to do.

CHAPTER 14

ANNIVERSARY IN HAWAII? NO - BRAZIL!

March, 1999 was our 30th wedding anniversary and Carol's mom wanted to do something special for us, like a vacation to Maui or Tahiti or something exciting like that. She didn't understand what we were doing and, being a world traveler herself, she really didn't understand not being able to see the sights when I went somewhere like Columbia, Argentina, Australia, or Brazil. "Well, didn't you at least get to see the Iguacu Falls between Argentina and Brazil?" She just couldn't understand that our trips consisted of the hotel, the church, and a restaurant. With Randy, Ben and I, it was a mission - we literally didn't have time for sightseeing. So, she wanted to do something nice for our 30th, but Carol told her what she really, really wanted was to go on the upcoming trip to Brazil. Randy was going to be taking a team and she was tired of hearing about the stories I told upon returning from one of these trips - she wanted to be part of it. Carol's mom reluctantly agreed and she put the cost of the airfare on her credit card, $750. Guess what? The bill never did show up on her card, and she is one who is meticulous at record keeping. She is still convinced to this day that somebody else got charged and just didn't catch it. We checked every way possible, and the charge just wasn't made. Was it a blessing from heaven? That's what we think.

In September, 1999 we took off for Londrina, Brazil before going back to Sao Paulo. Back in 1998 we had met Mike Shea, an American missionary who had been in Brazil about 14 years at that time. He was pastoring a small work, but really he was a strategist, an intercessor, a pastor to the pastors of that city, and a network-er, and he would soon form a worship team called Casa De Davi

(House of David). That team's worship music has now swept Brazil with a new sound, and they are influencing the entire country. It was Mike who arranged for many pastors and churches to come together and had rented a building that would hold 45,000 people where we would have five days of meetings. Randy had assembled quite a team to go on this trip.

MISSION POSSIBLE

This is how I filed the first report from Brazil:

"Your mission, should you choose to accept it, Mr Clark, is to once again infiltrate Brazil with the gospel. Thus began another missionary trip for Randy Clark and his 'Mission Possible' team. If you know Randy, you know you can't give him anything important, because he'll lose it. Well, now, we can't find that message. It's like it just self-destructed and disappeared."

"Randy appointed Rick Stivers, a trusted veteran from past campaigns in Russia and Argentina, as Chief-of-Staff. Rick, an insurance agent in his other life, is well known for his two training manuals on missionary trips, 'We Caught the Fire and Our Britches Are Still Burning' and 'There Are No Tacos In Argentina.' I will once again handle intelligence ("just the facts, ma'am," for the report). It was decided that we would send in four assaults, to land in timed waves in the key city of Sao Paulo."

"The first contingency gathered in Atlanta. It consisted of some wily veterans of past campaigns, such as me and my wife Carol, Bill and Barbara Cassada from New

Jersey, who had a year of similar missionary insurgencies with Randy as they traveled with him for a year, and Rex and Lois Burgher from Montana, who were with us in Brazil in March. We also brought new recruits - Errol Faulkes, pastor of the Albuquerque Vineyard, and two of his trusted lieutenants, Barbara Martin and Greg Shirley. Our plane landed in Sao Paulo at 6:30 AM, Monday morning and we immediately began touring (I mean, scouting) the airport. Once secured, and with our base camp set up at McDonalds, we awaited the next contingency."

"At 9:05am, the second plane arrived carrying Rick and his crew. This included Jerry and Cindy Bryant, Vineyard pastors from Nashville. Jerry is a seasoned veteran from our trip in March, and goes back with Randy to his Baptist days. Fresh recruits from California included Dave and Deborah Crone, who pastor a great Assemblies of God church in Vacaville, and David Metcalfe from San Jose. David is a policeman, so we brought him along 'in case of trouble.'"

"The next flight arrived at 9:18am from New York carrying John and Mellie MacKenzie. This couple is very experienced in deliverance, and they are also veterans of the March trip. I have to admit, we were pressing the timing a little bit, as these two groups didn't arrive until we were in the final stages of boarding our flight to Londrina, the site of our first meetings."

It was then that we learned that our commander and his trusty sidekick (intern) Ben Scofield wouldn't make it in today - something about a flight getting canceled. I think Randy just wanted to see how his troops would handle the situation. Off we went to Londrina to meet our host, Mike Shea.

There was a greeting party waiting for us at the airport. That was really special. Mike took us to a Churrascaria for lunch and then to the hotel for some rest before we needed to get ready for the first evening meeting. No one was in charge, but we all knew the Holy Spirit was going to give a message to someone!

WHO'S IN CHARGE?

"Our leader didn't show up, but God did!" That's what Rex said about that first meeting. Our whole time in Londrina was very prophetic, and it started immediately. Thirsty, the first thing Barbara C. did upon entering the building was to grab a bottle of water. A moment later, she spilled the water, and it had all run out. She felt it was a prophetic sign that God wanted to pour out His Spirit on all Londrina, and she used Ezekiel 47 to illustrate the point. It was only then that we found out the theme of this conference - "The River of God in Londrina." Ok, so we were off to a good start.

Dave Crone ended up having the message for the night. He shared how he had come to a place of intimately worshipping the Lord, and he felt there were many pastors and leaders who had not yet fully embraced all that God had for them. He talked about how, three years earlier, he felt God telling him to come to the front and passionately worship Him - only God told him to crawl to the front. After futile arguing with God, he did and it broke something in him. Some 300+ rushed to the front altar area and we began ministering to them for the rest of the evening. It was a powerful start to the conference.

The next morning, I had two realizations. Mike Shea had assembled a worship team, led by Davi Silva. Davi had been born with Down 's syndrome at a time when not much was known about that in Brazil. His mother had prayed, "Lord, either heal him or take him home. If he's still here tomorrow, I'm going to assume you will heal him." He was still there the next day and for 6 years she prayed faithfully. Then one day the special school he went to called her to tell her that he acted like a normal boy. Tests confirmed that he had absolutely no signs of Down's Syndrome in his chromosomes, although he still has some of the physical characteristics of it, like having only one line in the palm, etc. God's hand was on him and he became a very gifted worship leader.

My first realization? "Wow, this worship is REALLY good, and the leader is awesome."

WORSHIP WASHES OVER ME

Now, as Randy's scribe, many times the only time I had to write was during the next meeting. As I was sitting in the back writing a report of the previous evening, I suddenly realized that although I hadn't recognized any of the songs, and I certainly didn't understand the language, I felt like waves of beautiful worship were washing over me. Many times I didn't get to participate in the worship because I was writing, but this day worship came to me. It was as if God was saying, "It's okay, I am with you, even in the back of the hall while you're working."

After the morning meeting, we went off to a Chinese restaurant where the owner of the restaurant hosted us. Interestingly, he wasn't even a believer. When he heard about this event, he wanted to do something for us. Imagine. By then, Randy and Ben had joined us, so we got to pray for the owner before leaving. Just a special serendipity.

The next morning we were two hours into worship when prophetic things began to pop. Mike Shea was lying on the platform singing over and over, "He's the only thing we need." His wife joined him, and Deborah and Dave rushed up on the platform to lay hands on them. Connie (Mike's wife) and Deborah became a heap on the floor, and Mike was energized to sing as Dave prayed for him. Later, Mike was dancing over his wife and daughter, saying it was a symbolic act of how Jesus dances over His bride. He pointed at Dave and Deborah and prophesied the House of David over them. Down they went in a heap under the weight of those words. Next, Mike told of how, when David Yonngi Cho from South Korea came to Argentina for a conference, some Brazilians asked him to pray for Brazil. He said the Brazilian church was like a lion asleep, but, when it awakes, it will roar and it will be heard all around the earth. It has been prophesied that as the Iguaçu Falls is 12 times larger than Niagara Falls, so would the outpouring of the Holy Spirit be 12 times greater than that in Toronto! Most of us who have been to Brazil believe there is a powerful revival coming to the church in Brazil, and that they will be a catalyst to bring revival to the nations.

Randy finally came to the platform after 3 hours of worship that morning. He simply said that what we had just engaged in may have seemed undignified to some, that it may have even pushed their comfort zones. But often times just before the victory, God asks us to do something that doesn't make sense. The story of Gideon was a perfect example. We finished that morning session praying for everyone there, mostly pastors and leaders. It was a powerful morning, and the conference was gaining steam.

A HEALING CLINIC

Obviously, most of the meetings focused on healing. One morning, Randy taught on how to recognize words of knowledge for healing. The size of the group had now grown, even in the morning meetings, with about 4,000 turning up at night. We had 46 people get words for the first time and many people were healed. But that morning God wanted to put an emphasis on the teaching. Randy had gotten a pretty severe pain in his back and he knew it was for hips, back and spinal pain. Forty people responded to that word. He had them line up facing the congregation. As Randy prayed for them a general prayer, many began to be affected by the power of the Spirit. It became a clinic, as Randy would describe what to look for as the Spirit - many were crowded up front to see. Five were sovereignly healed, right in front of everyone. One of the testimonies was of a woman who had been experiencing such severe pain all down her left side for last eight years that she couldn't even sit down without pain and now it had all gone. As she was testifying, the power of God hit her again and she began jumping and dancing around, something she definitely hadn't been able to do before.

All the teaching in the world couldn't have better demonstrated what happened next. As the fire of God hit one woman and healed her right in front of all of us, it also hit a woman in a wheelchair. As Randy began praying for her, she shook wildly. Polio had confined her to that chair. One man began shaking violently and crashed to the floor - he had been trying to tell Mike that he had a vision for her. Randy had him pray for her, and I, for one, was thinking, "This is so God - we're about to see a miracle right in front of us!"

She wanted to stand up. Now, Randy never tries to pull anyone up from a wheelchair, but, if they want to stand up, he honors that request. Every one of the 200+ people gathered around were believing for a miracle, and I wish I could tell you it happened, but it didn't. Randy completed the teaching for that morning by talking about how the healing ministry was about entering into the suffering of others and showing them the love and compassion of Jesus. Randy was able to use this experience as a great example on how we need to keep pressing in for more of the anointing of God, because what we had wasn't enough. When we don't see the blind see, or the cripple walk, this should drive us to draw closer to Him, to contend with Him for "more."

HEALING STORIES — LIKE STUTTERING

That night, Randy didn't get out of the meeting until 10 PM, later than he would have liked. But we all sensed that the power of God would be evident to those who would stay and press in. It was a somewhat chaotic meeting, in that he told everyone who felt the power of God on them during the message to stand, so that he could bless them. Then we would interview those who had been healed while he continued to preach. This testimony brought the house down. A young woman named Marcia was with her two friends. They all got healed. Marcia had stuttered all her life, and had been crying out to God for the past five years for her healing. Of course, by now we're all realizing she is talking perfectly normally, as her voice raised to praise God who has healed her. This is what I wrote it in the report I filed, "Just imagine how amazed and happy you'd be if you had stuttttered (this was actually a typing accident, but it was like a prophetic sign so I left it in) all your life, and now, in the twinkling of an eye, sovereignly, you were healed!"

We had some incredible stories of healings come out of these meetings, of which these are just a few. Dave C. prayed for a 37 year old man who had been hurt in an accident when he was a kid and, as a result, was almost completely blind in the right eye. Vision out of it was very fuzzy and cloudy, and he couldn't distinguish anyone's features, even up close. Dave said he prayed very simply, and within about 10 seconds the vision began improving. He prayed again and the man said, "I can see people!"

Rick talked to a pastor named Zinaldo. He and his wife were at home listening to one of the services on the radio. They wanted to expose their 78 year old neighbor to the gospel, so they took their radio down to her apartment and listened to the service together. She had not been able to walk without her walker for years, but when they started to pray for the sick in the service, she wanted to get up and walk. They prayed for her, and she was able to take baby steps. She got better and better and wouldn't stop. About that time the nurse came to check in on her and exclaimed, "She can't do that!" The pastor preached the gospel to both of them and they got saved!

At the same time, I got the name "Marta" during worship and had the impression of "female problems." Out of all the translators I could have asked, I happened to ask Jussara, who told me it was a common name (I wanted to see if I was hearing from God). She knew that the woman who was catering the food for our team was named Marta and that she had just had a baby, and had lost the previous pregnancy before this birth. I thought this was more than just a coincidence. Later, during ministry time, there was Marta. She had pain in her uterus, kidney stones, and pain in her neck. I prayed for her and watched as God took all the pain out of those areas. I had been asking God for the gift to receive not only of words of knowledge, but to receive the person's name as well. This was a beginning.

On the last night I prayed for a woman who had fallen two months before and hurt her left shoulder. She couldn't lift it at all, and she was in pain. As I came against an afflicting spirit, you could see it leave and the healing come. She began to move her arm all around and there was no pain.

Jerry Bryant would continually amaze us with his accuracy in words of knowledge. In hindsight, I now know his gift is very much like the way William Branham used to move in or like the way Todd Bentley moves today. In one of the meetings, Jerry had "seen" that a man had been electrocuted and that it had caused pain and withering in his arm. That's exactly what had happened to a man, and when he responded to the word of knowledge he was completely healed! All the pain left and he had complete mobility in his arm again.

We had more unusual stories. Deborah had prayed for a woman who suffered from tormenting dreams. That night she was once again tormented, but she had been told about her authority in Christ. She told the spirit to leave and proclaimed that she would only have God dreams, but she had another troubling dream. At first she thought it was demonic, but the Holy Spirit told her to intercede, and she did. She had dreamed of a plane trying to land, skidding off the runway, and breaking into three pieces. The next morning she heard the news that a plane with about 250 on board in Spain had crashed, it had broken into three pieces, but no one was seriously hurt. Another one of those things that makes you wonder. Coincidence? I don't know - but very interesting!

BACK TO THE
FOURSQUARE CHURCH IN SAO PAULO

With about three hours of sleep, we took off the next morning to Sao Paulo to continue this mission. We would be meeting in the Foursquare church we had first visited in March. Additionally, we were expecting to have a large crusade type meeting with the Foursquare denomination, which was having a convention in Sao Paulo at that time, but we were soon to find that it was not to be.

We walked in that night to their regular Sunday night service and noted the change in worship immediately. We moved from a rocking, yet very intimate style of worship to one of high praise, with a choir and a praise team. Different, but wonderful! After a great message and many people getting saved or rededicated, we moved into a time for words of knowledge for healing. Jerry continued to amaze us. He "saw" a picture of someone falling into a well and hurting their back. A man found him later and said that is exactly what had happened to him.

As Randy prayed over the room for those who had responded to the words, we saw 45 healed. Then a man came up to him and said he felt that if Randy would wave over the congregation, there would be another wave of healing. I had gotten the same impression, but hadn't told Randy because I had thought that it was just a memory of the same thing happening the previous time. Randy went for it and waved over the room. Almost immediately, the healing increased and soon there were 117 healed!

The meetings were being broadcast over the radio and Dave C. said, "The airwaves are electronic handkerchiefs." There had been so much response the night before that it had overwhelmed the one person who was handling the incoming phone calls - they had to add six more people. One woman called to say her severely crossed eyes had completely straightened, and we had many more people come to the meetings because of what they had heard on the radio. It's just amazing to me what the proclamation of the word will produce. It's a biblical revelation.

"I'M NOT LEAVING UNTIL I'M HEALED!"

Next we went into words of knowledge for healing. It was this night that God gave Carol a higher level of anointing for physical healing. It's an incredible story of healing - one which we constantly tell even now. To set the scene, understand that Carol had many apprehensions about going on this trip, one of which was, "Will I be used for physical healing, or will I be like a bump on a log in the midst of all these anointed people?" Carol was known for being much anointed in the issues of the heart. Her gift was inner healing, but she had rarely ever gotten a word of knowledge for healing. Now she had already been used on this trip for physical healing, but this is the one story that made the most impact; this is where she had the "ahaaa, I've got it."

I got a word of knowledge for "fuzzy or blurred vision." A woman came up to Carol later when we went into a time of ministry of praying for the sick. She said she had responded to my word, but had not been healed. She had severe astigmatism for 30 years and wore "coke-bottle thick glasses" (someone pointed out to us that many young people under 20 aren't familiar with that term, so, for them - they used to sell coke in bottles and the bottom was very thick, hence the term). When she took off her glasses, even from about five feet away she couldn't tell if you were a man or a woman, black or white. She said, "I came determined to get healed, I didn't get healed during the prayer for the words given, and I'm not leaving tonight until I'm healed!"

Now Carol did what many of you would have done. She was saying to herself, "Oh God, oh God, oh God - I told you I wanted something easy! Why did she come to me? Anyone but me! Where's Randy, where's Bill? Anyone but me." But there was this person in front of her, and Carol responded to the need. She laid hands on the woman's eyes and began to pray. After a couple of minutes, she stopped and checked in with her. The woman said she thought her eyes were about 20% better. Once again, Carol did what many would do - "Really?" She prayed some more, checking in with her every couple of minutes. The woman's eyes continued to get better and better, and after about 20 minutes she could clearly read the clock on the back wall, which neither of us could read! Best of all, she could no longer see with her glasses. When Randy asked the next night if anyone wanted to testify of a dramatic healing, she was the first to respond - and she wasn't wearing her glasses!

KIDNEY STONE PASSES – OUCH

That night was the last night at this Foursquare church, and it was a "blowout." We had already had the testimony above. Another woman had received prayer for severe kidney stone pain and had passed it during the night with no pain, despite its size – ouch! A young man with bronchitis since childhood didn't "feel" anything during prayer, but in the morning he had exercised and had run and run - something he definitely hadn't been able to do before. When Randy went for words of knowledge, the baton had been passed to the Brazilians. The US team hardly got any words - it was the Brazilians, and they were accurate words. Many got healed during the prayer.

The US team wasn't through with healing for the night. Toward the end of the evening, Deborah and Barbara M. were asked to pray for a woman who could only come as far as the lobby. She was in such pain from an automobile wreck that she had to be carried in on a chair and couldn't even be touched. They led her to the Lord, took care of some demonic stuff, and then prayed for healing. Her leg had been so damaged that she had to drag it and had to use a walker. After prayer her entire countenance had changed, she was able to walk, and all the pain had left! She had been brought by a woman who had a stony heart and they could tell that she was anxious to leave. Deborah began to bless her, and began to "read her mail" and prophesy over her - she walked out a new woman. Oh, the power of prophesy. Finally, as they came out into the lobby, they ran into a family they recognized from Londrina. They prayed for the daughter, who was completely deaf in her left ear. As soon as they laid hands on her, she went out under the power of the Spirit. Afterwards, they plugged up the good ear, whispered in the left ear, and watched as her face lit up. She could hear!

THIS CHURCH DIDN'T REALLY WANT US

From this Foursquare Church, we moved on the next day to a large and very influential Assemblies of God Church. The pastor, who wasn't in town at the time, was the head of the pastors' association, which was about 2,000 strong. There were a lot of things going on politically at the Foursquare church, and it was probably better that we didn't know about at the time. These meetings had been arranged with about a week's notice. At this same time, the Foursquare denomination was having a large meeting and Randy and the team were supposed to lead some meetings there. Not all of the leadership was in favor of that, however, and in fact, right after we left to return home, they voted and the Foursquare leader who had just hosted us was voted out of his office. So, instead of Randy speaking at the conference, it was arranged for us to go to this AG church. What we didn't know was they weren't very open to the "Toronto" move.

When we arrived for the morning meeting we discovered the church occupied an old beer distributor building. It held more than 3,000 people and there would be at least that many there that night for their regular Wednesday night meeting. For this first morning there were about 175. The building had a concrete floor, with a little carpet down front, a tin roof, and it was open at the end of the room opposite the platform. It also allowed vehicles to drive in at that end, so while you were speaking or ministering from the platform, you could see cars coming in. You would probably never see something like that in the US, but it seemed to work down there. Randy gave a great encouraging message about "leaving your comfort zone" for the things of God, and then went for healing. It was hard plowing and they didn't receive or seem to be as "into" it as in the last two places, but God showed Himself strong and set the course for the next two days. During the ministry time, Eviny received prayer for the deafness in her left ear she had had for 10 years. Before the prayer, if you covered the good ear, she could tell you were speaking, but couldn't understand the words. Now she could hear perfectly. And Randy prayed for a man who had been completely deaf in his left ear for 38 years. After prayer, he could plug up his good ear and now hear a whisper out of the left ear!

THE EARS HAVE IT

With these cases of ears being healed, that evening Randy felt like there was a special anointing for ear problems and deafness. With the words of knowledge we saw 91 people get healed, 18 of which were related to deafness or ear problems! There's a key here - always pay attention to what God is doing. Then, when we went into ministry time at the end, we saw another 67 healed.

It was an interesting scenario. We had about 3,000 people in this service, no heat (and it was definitely cool that night with one end of the building being open) and only 15 of the team members present, as several weren't feeling well. When Randy said we would pray for the sick at the end of the service, it felt like 2,000 stayed and lined up. Randy said we would have to pray for two at a time. When we finally gathered back together at 2 AM to confer about what had happened, we all said that everyone we had prayed for got healed. We couldn't pray for all 2,000, but everyone we did pray for got healed!

Interestingly, as we began the time of ministry, the first five people who came to Carol had problems with astigmatism! Randy loves it when a "little ole me" gets anointed. He especially likes it when it's the least likely you would think of - like a former Presbyterian pastor who has been seminary trained. Like Carol. Randy told the story of the woman with severe astigmatism getting healed at the last church when Carol prayed for her, so five people who had the same type problem had made a bee line for her during prayer - and they all got healed!

The next day was the last of this ministry trip. Randy taught in the morning on the model for healing and how to recognize words of knowledge, and then had the Brazilians pray for those who had needs. It was the "passing of the baton," which has become a hallmark of Randy's Global Awakening ministry, and continues to this day. Leaving a deposit behind has become a very important component of Randy's ministry. On this trip, we were able to determine from first-hand accounts that there was a deposit left during the March meetings in Sao Paulo, as many of the people testified that they saw an increase in the numbers of healings as they took the training and impartation back with them to their churches.

Another thing happened on this trip that has continued to happen on every one of Randy's trips to this day – every single person on the team experienced people getting healed when they prayed, and every single person started moving in the gift of words of knowledge. Additionally, for those of the team members who already moved in the gifting of words of knowledge and healing, the anointing seemed to go up even higher.

A GLOBAL AWAKENING RESOURCE TEAM

In looking back, we realize this was a turning point for us in our ministry. There was a tremendous anointing that came on Carol for physical healing and words of knowledge for healing, and we discovered that there was grace on us, especially on Carol, for the grueling schedule of a ministry trip like this. Carol had been worried that she wouldn't get enough sleep, not get enough protein, and that God wouldn't use her like He used the others. All doubts proved to be false, and she didn't even crash when we returned home - she wasn't just running on high energy.

This trip also seemed to solidify us in Randy's eyes as a future Resource Team. I had already told Randy that we wanted to continue to do this type of ministry, and we had already determined that we would travel with him through November, but there had not been a firm commitment of what would happen after we stopped traveling. On one of the lunch breaks on this trip, Randy spoke with both of us, confirmed that he indeed considered us as one of his teams after we stopped traveling, and that on the last trip, when all the associates and those close to his ministry came together, he would ordain us.

When I began traveling with Randy, it was just such a thrill to be part of his ministry that I didn't have a long-range game plan. I had wanted to pray for the sick, teach on healing and impart this gift to others, but I never saw how that could happen. When I became part of Randy's ministry, part of that desire was fulfilled. I quickly saw that once I stopped traveling, there was a need for the type of ministry that his Resource Teams did and I wanted to do that, but I didn't know if that would happen. Now, we were pointing to making that dream a reality.

CHAPTER 15

"CATCH THE FIRE" -
TORONTO AND SPOKANE

October was broken up into two trips. The first was back to Toronto for the 1999 "Catch the Fire Conference." It started out as a conference of "gold" and "Brazilians." We had seen the gold dust and gold teeth in Brazil on last month's trip. Then, on returning to San Diego, we went to a conference, led by Carlos Annacondia, where many received new gold teeth. When we got to Toronto we found it was happening there also and had been for the previous few months. John Arnott started the meeting by praying over the crowd of about 3,000 for God to give gold teeth to those who needed dental work. A Brazilian woman came to show a row of brilliant gold fillings she had gotten during that prayer. John then called up the delegation of about 125 Brazilians who had come to the conference, and we got to pray for them. This was particularly special because we had met many of that delegation at the meetings we had just done in Brazil. It was great prayer time and a great start to the conference. One man was speaking English from the floor, and I confirmed he knew no English!

Randy then entered into team ministry, and had me, Ben, Rex and Lois share about the recent trip. I told the story of getting the word for fuzzy, blurred vision and Carol praying for this woman with such severe astigmatism that she couldn't tell if you were man or woman, black or white from three feet away without her glasses - and she was totally healed!

Ben's story was encouraging because it had some very important points in it. He had gotten the opportunity to pray for a woman in a meeting the night he returned from Brazil. She was deaf in both ears and couldn't even hear the band. She and her husband were reluctant for her to get prayer, because by this time she had gotten a lot prayer with no results. They didn't want to be disappointed again, nor did they want Ben to get discouraged. They just didn't know how much faith he was carrying. He convinced them to receive prayer, and then just watched as the power of God came on her after about a minute, and her ears opened up. And this was in the US! We've just got to get over that thing that says these kinds of things only happen in Third World countries, that they have more faith, that they don't have the advantages of medicine and science, etc. I've heard it said that it's not that the people in Brazil, China or India have more faith - it's that they have *less unbelief* - and I believe that. You don't have to convince many other cultures about the reality of spiritual forces. Unfortunately, the Western mindset is one of unbelief, and we've got to break through that.

FIRST MIRACLE
RANDY ONLY SPEAKS 15 MINUTES

After our stories, there was great faith in the room. Randy went for words of knowledge for healing. Within 20 minutes there were 235 healed from conditions these words described. Then, probably the greatest miracle of the evening occurred - he only spoke for 15 minutes! Randy felt he was to give some of his testimony over the next few days to encourage many who were weary, much as he had been before God touched him in the fall of '93. As such, Randy had all the pastors and their spouses come up to the area behind the platform so that he and his team could pray for them, while the rest of the conference attendees received refreshing from the prayer team. It was also a time of healing. Since we had seen so many deaf healed in recent meetings, he told the conference that the team would begin praying for anyone with ear problems at 11 PM (remember, the anointing always goes up after 11). Again, the anointing was very evident. While Randy was praying for the pastors, he got a severe pain in his ears. When he asked if anyone around him had that problem, two responded. One man was so deaf that he had to rely on reading lips. Both were completely healed! All told, we saw many healed of hearing problems. We left that night around 12:30, feeling as though it were a great start to the conference.

THE POWER OF THE TESTIMONY

One of the highlights of every meeting in Toronto is the testimony. This conference was no exception. John Arnott had a woman come up who had been touched while there in 1995. All her Christian life, her church had preached against dancing. As a result, coming to Toronto was a stretch for her. She didn't say why she had come, but maybe it was because she was so desperate - she had tuberculosis. During the worship one night in '95, she heard the Lord say to tear off a tag on her jeans. She had wanted to ignore this, because it sounded so silly, but finally she went in the bathroom and tore the tag off the jeans. They had been made in China and she could read the tag - it was a curse. Now, did that cause you to go look at your jeans - be honest now! As she took the tag off, she threw it on the floor and began dancing on it. John Arnott saw her later and thought she was a professional ballerina, her dancing was so graceful. Of course, all the symptoms of tuberculosis were gone, along with the pain. She had been x-rayed many times since then and nothing showed up. Her doctor couldn't explain it, but said she was healed! As we went into worship before the speaker came up, she began to dance, and it was the most graceful dancing you've ever seen.

That night was once again about healing. After the speaker told many stories of the healing they had seen in Toronto, he had Randy and the team come up to give words of knowledge. Then we went into a time of ministry for healing. In the last two weeks since we had all been home from Brazil, Randy and Ben had seen 8 people completely healed from deafness. That night, two Korean women had their deaf ears completely open to hear. We were in a season where a lot of deaf people were getting healed and we wondered if the prophetic people would say God was trying to say something to His people - perhaps that He wanted their ears to be open to hear? Hmmmmmmm.

LIVING EXAMPLES OF HIS TEACHING

The Friday night meeting was to be Randy's last meeting at this conference. He had a short message that was burning in him and it had God's anointing on it. He called up all those who were in itinerant ministry and all those pastors who had set up their churches to be places dedicated to sending people out. He had the 150+ people who responded come up and face the congregation, and the he made an apostolic call for all those pastors who God was now calling to make similar declarations - that they would be willing "to go" and "to send." More people flooded toward the front and Randy released us to pray for them. While this was happening, he gave a passionate explanation of what it means "to go." He explained that there is a cost and a sacrifice but the rewards in lives changed makes it all worth it. He used people like me, Rex and Lois, and Bob Bradbury as examples of people who had considered the cost and made a sacrifice to follow God, no matter what. He pointed out that we were all there at our own expense and that God had honored that sacrifice. I had gotten the chance to travel around the world and had seen many lives touched by the power of God. Bob was being used powerfully with youth, and Rex and Lois were now entering that trail. It was one of the wildest nights I had ever witnessed.

SO MUCH PAIN, SHE MISSED
FIRST 4 DAYS OF THE CONFERENCE

Since I knew I might not be back to Toronto any time soon, I wanted to enjoy my stay, and decided to stay through Sunday night.

Randy came to the church with me Saturday morning before leaving, and we encountered some of the Korean friends we had made on May trip there. They wanted us to pray for this Korean woman who had made the long trip there to the conference, only to be so sick and in so much pain that she had not been able to get out of bed for the first four days of the conference. She had suffered with severe arthritis for many years and the 22 hour trip had taken its toll on her body and health. Randy literally had only five minutes to pray with her, but I said I would keep praying. You could tell she was very uncomfortable because of the pain, and she seemed very cold and indifferent to the brief prayer.

I saw her later that night and learned she still felt achy all over her body. As I prayed for her, I also had several of the Koreans around her begin to pray. The Holy Spirit hit like a bomb on these prayer warriors and then the power flowed into her. I felt like I was to get her up and have her walk. You could literally see her beginning to get better as she walked. It was like there was oil flowing throughout all her body, lubricating all the joints. I left her on the floor with no pain. The next morning they brought her to me after the service - all bright, shiny and with no pain. Now her request was, "Pray for me to be anointed - I want to take this healing power and anointing back with me." That's what it's all about, eh?

There are so many lessons in this story aren't there? First of all, she "came." The huge majority of the time in the gospels, those who were healed "came" to Jesus (just think about Jairus, the woman with the issue of blood, the leper, the Gadarene demoniac, etc). She was desperate for her healing, even when the enemy threw obstacles at her. She got prayed for by several people, several times, and it wasn't always by the "anointed man of faith and power for the hour." (Randy hates that label and that's why his teaching on "God Can Use Little Ole Me" is so important).

STAYIN' IN THE RIVER

One of the themes of this particular conference was about "staying in the river." Melinda Fish gave a great message that Saturday night, entitled "Don't Be Tellin' Me This Ain't God." It was an encouraging message to stay in the river and to guard against a "been there, done that" kind of attitude. Everyone needes to hear that message, and unfortunately many have not heeded it, have drifted to try to find something else, or have thought the river dried up and now it's back to life as normal. I think what is important is to realize that God has *never* stopped renewing His church, and He never will. There were still new people coming into the river in 1999, just as there are now.

Fifteen year old Ashley proved my point on that night. The ministry time was one of "soaking" in the love of the Father. As a ministry team member that night, I approached her as she was standing in line to receive prayer. Her look said, "Go ahead, you can pray, but nothing's going to happen." As the joy of the Lord hit her, her eyes opened wide in surprise, and she tumbled to the floor. We got her up and prayed for her several times more and soaked her. She literally staggered out under the weight of the Father's love.

This "staying in the river" was brought to my attention even more the next morning at the regular Sunday service. John Arnott spoke pointedly and passionately about this subject. At one point he asked how many had been there on those first 4 days in January, 1994, and a few raised their hands. A woman right in front of me who had raised her hand, told me she had been on the worship team on the second night. Amazingly, when John invited all who had become dry or were no longer in the river of God like they would like to be, she went forward for prayer. In retrospect, now 8 years removed from that day, I think one of our biggest struggles is to stay in that passionate place where we desire God more than life itself - as Heidi Baker says, to be "laid down lovers."

NEW SHOES AND A NEW
CARRIER OF THE GLORY

My time in Toronto finished with the Healing Service they had on Sunday nights. As usual, they started with testimonies. One woman was from Cork, Ireland. There had been a word of knowledge in one of Randy's meetings for TMJ, but she hadn't been there. I got to pray for her the next day. I could hear the bones and jaw grinding as though they were being reset in the proper place. She told me Sunday night that all the pain was gone and she had been able to sleep for the past two nights, something she hadn't been able to do for years. As a bonus, God had healed her longstanding back pain that morning.

There was also this testimony. A woman from London showed the congregation assembled her shoes, which were built up with a special heel. She had a hip problem that had, since birth, caused one leg to be more than 1 ¼ inch shorter than the other. On Wednesday night, she got healed and had to go out and buy regular shoes to wear for the first time ever!

I met a young woman named Dagmar, who had come over from Germany with nine other friends. I prayed for all of them, but when I got to her, nothing happened. Usually, you at least see "something" happening - maybe an eyelid fluttering a little or something. But after about 20 minutes of my best prayers, she said she had felt absolutely nothing. I asked two of the regular prayer team members to come and soak her, and they were eager to oblige. Yeah, that's the ticket - let the professionals do the job. But, when they finished after about 20 minutes, there was still nothing. It was then that God spoke to me that she was a "carrier of the glory." There were two women nearby and I asked them if she could pray for them under my supervision. They said yes. When the first assumed the position, as soon as Dagmar touched the woman on her palm with her finger, she started vibrating and down she went. You should have seen Dagmar's eyes as they widened in surprise. The same thing happened when she prayed for the other. I explained to her that she was a "carrier of the glory." By that I mean, she didn't have to "shake and bake," she didn't have to have the manifestations that some other people had, but she did carry His presence with her.

Later, I found out she prayed for one the women's friends, who had a physical affliction, and she was instantly healed as Dagmar prayed! I saw her the next day before going home and she said, "My friends told me on the way over to Toronto 'we don't know why you're going - God can't use you if you don't feel anything.' Now I know! I'm a carrier of the glory, and I'm going back to Germany to lay hands on everything that moves!" Another "little ole me" set loose - this time in Germany.

HEALING ROOMS GRAND OPENING

The next time I was with Randy was when he and Bill Johnson were to be the speakers at the grand opening of the Spokane Healing Rooms. Cal Pierce had left the church in Redding, heading for Spokane without really knowing why. It soon became clear as he got a vision for re-opening the Healing Rooms established by John G. Lake. From 1915 to 1920, it is said that they had over 100,000 documented healings and the US government said that it was the "healthiest city in the US." Cal Pierce actually found the same rooms that had been used back then, rented them, and reopened them. This conference was to celebrate this ministry - and there was power in those rooms. During the conference, they opened the rooms for anyone who wanted to go through them. We went into a room and "soaked" for about an hour. When we got up to leave, a man, who had taken his glasses off while lying on the floor, put them back on, only to realize that he couldn't see. He took them off again, and realized that he had been healed - healed in an hour, with no one praying for him.

Randy did the normal teachings he was known for; he taught on healing, words of knowledge for healing, and he talked about impartation. The impartation is always there because he not only teaches on it and does it, but others get released to do the same. Many got words of knowledge that led to someone's healing for the first time. The next day, we met with about 150 pastors and leaders for a lunchtime of questions with Randy and Bill. Someone asked about the lack of authority in the church to set the captives free. This gave Randy an opportunity to launch out on the ministry of Carlos Annacondia, and the success he was having around the world. Another question was, "How do you get your people to get hungry for revival?" Both Randy and Bill explained that they focus on those who are hungry, and try to get a breakthrough on someone who is reluctant to the move of God, because that will provoke the others when there is a breakthrough. And Randy said something really interesting. He said, "The Holy Spirit has a greater capacity to enjoy diversity than I do."

I have had to lean on both of those insights fairly often since then. Many times we have done meetings, and I haven't seen or sensed the hunger in the people. Then I just go after those who **are** hungry - but I always remember that if someone had seen me prior to that fateful meeting in Carol's church that night in 1992, they would not have seen a very hungry, desperate person. All things are possible. I don't try to judge who will be touched, but I'm always aware of the hungry. I'm also aware that as we continue in this present move of God, there will always be some who question if it's God, and if God would really do that to a person. I just keep Randy's comment about the Holy Spirit's capacity to enjoy diversity in mind.

I LEARNED THE OUTCOME 7 YEARS LATER

In the last evening meeting that Randy was able to attend, I witnessed a clear demonstration of desperation. While talking about the principle of faith, a man named Bill got up and said, "I'm desperate for more anointing right now, but I might not be in 15 minutes. Would you pray for me?" As Randy prayed for him, I caught him and then "soaked" him for the rest of the message. He told me later he couldn't **not** go forward - with electricity still flowing through him, he told me that he believed he had been empowered to "go," which he had been crying out for.

After Randy left, Bill Johnson took over for the next two days, and I stayed. Several things came out of that. First, a man named Todd gave his testimony. He had cancerous tumors in his body and had been in constant pain for the past three years. The pain got so bad that six months before they implanted a morphine pump in him to control the pain, but it didn't help. On the first night I prayed for him, and he had been pain free now for four days! He got "soaked" in prayer and *knew* something had happened to him. But, of course, he went home to Idaho after the conference, and I went on with my life. I didn't find out what had happened to him until November, 2005. He saw me at Randy Clark's conference in Harrisburg. He rushed up to me with this huge smile on his face. "Hi, do you remember me?" Not really - we had met a lot of people in the past eight years and had prayed for a lot of people. He reminded me, and said, "I'm not supposed to be here, according to the doctors, but here I am!"

Once again, the point is that we all are going to pray for people and may never know what the effects of those prayers are until heaven. Here's something else I've learned – I don't always know what happens when I pray for someone, but I believe that something happens every time I pray. It may not manifest for some time, and that's where the enemy often has a field day. He tries to convince us we didn't get healed, that nothing happened. Lately, though, more and more people have come up to us - sometimes weeks later, sometimes years later - and they have testified of how God healed them or touched them in some unique way.

DR. PRICE PROPHECY

Bill also shared something that I had never heard, and it has been something that I was to hold onto to use later whenever the move of God wasn't going like I thought it should, or whenever our ministry took a downturn. Bill shared about some visions that Dr. Charles Price had in 1947. He was a very educated man, was anti-healing and against the manifestations of the Spirit, but he got transformed in an Aimee Semple McPherson meeting, and was powerfully used by God.

In the first vision he saw a mighty revival, with many tents and fire coming out of them. This was the revival of the 1950's, when there were as many as 300 revival tents crisscrossing America. But man got his dirty little hands on it and God removed His hand. Then he saw revival come to the churches you wouldn't normally associate with revival - Catholics, Episcopalians, Presbyterians. This was the charismatic revival of the '60s-'70s, but it too was corrupted by man and died. But then he saw that before the trumpet of the Lord sounded, a revival started and spread from the East coast (Toronto to Pensacola?) to the West coast and then to the nations. This revival was so great that man couldn't get his dirty little hands on it. Prior to describing these visions, he had told his associates exactly when he would die and when his funeral would be - and he was right! So, perhaps we need to pay attention to what he was seeing. I keep hanging on to this and believe we are in the end-time revival - and it's not going away. It's not going to stop like previous revivals. I guess the question we have to ask is, "Will I stop?"

CHAPTER 16

THE LAST TRIP - NEW ENGLAND

AN UNUSUAL PRAYER
STYLE, BUT LOOK AT THE RESULTS

Now we came to November, 1999. This was the agreed-upon month when Carol and I had determined that we would stop traveling with Randy on a full-time basis. It had been in the Global Awakening meeting the previous October, 1998, when they had started talking about two meetings in New England, that something jumped in our hearts and we knew that it was important for us to be there. Randy would be doing meetings organized by about five churches in and around the New Haven, Connecticut area, but we were staying in this storybook little town called Old Saybrook, as guests of an Episcopal church. They, too, were involved in the meetings and would host the Global Awakening Associates meeting between conferences.

There were about 500 in attendance for the first night, about 95% of whom had never seen Randy. There was, and still is, so much misinformation about the "Toronto Blessing," so the Spirit had him ramble for a while that night. It totally disarmed those who had come fearing some "slick" evangelist. And how's this for an opening - he remembered something he had done back in 1995, something he had never done before or since:

Jenny had been in a car accident and had suffered brain damage. She couldn't walk for a year, couldn't talk much, and had lost much of her memory. She had been getting worse and the doctors had no hope for her. Randy remembered praying for her late one night back in '95 - remember, the anointing goes up after 11 PM. God impressed on him to put his forehead on hers, which he did for about 20 minutes. Just so you get the right picture of this, she was lying on her back, facing up. He was facing down, with his body stretched out the opposite way. Nothing inappropriate. Well, that night in November 1999, she was there to testify how she had been miraculously healed. Doesn't make sense does it? But then, neither does it sound logical when Jesus put mud in the eye of a blind man - but he was healed!

The second night Randy told his testimony. We had all heard this many times - after traveling with him 16 months, you can imagine how many times I had heard this - but we always laughed about it, and that night I heard more of an explanation than I had heard previously. In this testimony, he shares that being used by God to start the Toronto Blessing was not really about him, but about God's mercy and grace. By the time he was on the verge of a nervous breakdown in the fall of '93, he realized he had gotten away from what had been on his heart from God when he started the church in St. Louis. It had been birthed in signs and wonders and the power of God, but it had slowly drifted away from that over the years. It was not what Randy wanted when he found himself in the desert. He had told his associate pastor right before he went to the meetings with Rodney Howard Browne that he was "willing to lose half the church in order to get **Him** back." He had determined in his heart that he had to be true to what God had called him to be, no matter the cost. This night, he was challenging the people to be hungry, and the people flooded the altar area.

RANDY REALLY STRETCHES HIS TEAM

During one of the morning meetings, Randy furthered the whole team's education by casually mentioning that he thought there would be prophetic words from the team that morning. I know most of us thought, "That would be nice," but we weren't prepared for what was about to happen. After all, he was talking about how the prophetic words he had received before had helped him in his walk through this renewal.

At the end of his teaching, he had the team face the 150+ assembled, called upon Holy Spirit to touch them, and then told us to pick out those we could prophesy over. It was intimidating, but we did it and God backed us up. Most of us said afterwards that we usually didn't have much for the person, but as we would begin prophesying, the Lord would give more (probably a biblical principle in there, eh?). All I know is that there were bodies lying all over the floor and some people were shaking an hour later, or just couldn't get up. We all had stories like this: one woman I walked by during worship felt she heard God say He was going to give me something for her, and call her out. And I did. Another woman got prophesied to and had received a prophetic word three weeks before that there was another word coming for her. She wondered if that would be this day, and, sure enough, a team member called her out. Pretty amazing since none of us knew this was going to happen, including Randy!

CONSERVATISM HOLDS THEM BACK

Saturday night was to be the last night of this conference. The air was charged with electricity - we had reached breakthrough time. Randy preached on "Pressing In." There had only been three times since he had first given this message in 1995 when no one rushed him before the message was through. This night would be a repeat of what had become common - many were so drawn by God they were willing to go outside of their comfort zones and answer the hunger in their hearts. I watched as several were being drawn by the Spirit, but their conservatism kept them from coming forward.

Finally, one man could stand it no longer. He bolted to Randy in the middle of his message for him to lay hands on him. Randy often says it's not about what he can give anyone, but there is a biblical principle for the laying on of hands to stir up the anointing - and there were many who were hungry for more of God. When this man bolted, others followed and soon Randy was surrounded by a sea of hands reaching out to him for anointing. In these meetings, we saw a woman who had been full of fears a couple of days earlier press into God for more. A 17 year old girl saw the healing anointing go up significantly after we had laid hands on her. These were always great meetings, but you didn't usually get immediate feedback from anyone that told what had happened. Over time, though, there have been many reports of what God did. People like Heidi Baker, Leif Hetland, and Henry Maldava, a missionary in Honduras, the "fire man" of Brazil, and many of his travel companions and later interns.

HE'S GOING TO INVITE US TO
HIS CHURCH - HE JUST DOESN'T KNOW IT

This was also the start of a great friendship with Tom Ruotolo, who would later become the Vice President of the Global Awakening foreign trips. Tom was a Vineyard pastor and when he gave the announcements on Wednesday night, I felt like the Holy Spirit whispered to me that he would ask us to speak at his church on Sunday morning. That was amazing, since I had not yet met him!

Soon it was Saturday night and he hadn't asked. I thought maybe I had missed it, but at 11:30 he came to us and asked us to speak. That was one of the many times when it was needful to be ready, in season and out. Tom was hungry and he wanted it for his church. And his church was hungry too.

That Sunday morning we talked about the impartation of the gifts and of hunger. When we gave the altar call, 90% came forward with passion, many falling and groaning before they even got to the front. Afterwards, many said they had been dry and empty and needed to see the power of God back in their church. Once again, I got the chance to do what is most on my heart. We believe in equipping and Randy had taught us well. I prayed for two teenagers. They were really touched and I had them start praying with me, giving them pointers along the way, since this was the first time they had done this. They were amazed as the power of God would flow through them, and the people would fall out.

All of this touched Tom so much and ignited a fresh hunger in him that he just had to come to the next meetings, scheduled in Massachusetts. He just dropped everything and came, hoping to meet Randy. Randy always has a heart for young, hungry, desperate pastors, and Tom got to have some time with Randy during the meetings. As a result, he came on the September Brazil trip in 2000, and would later crisscross the world, coordinating trips for Randy and Global Awakening - even leading some of them.

WE GET "SENT OUT"

After these meetings, we gathered at the church in Old Saybrook for a couple of days as the Global Awakening team, associates, and friends gathered to pray, strategize and prepare for the coming year. It was a special time for Carol and I, as they laid hands on us and "sent us out." They also laid hands on Rex and Lois as they officially joined Global, and Rex began to travel with Randy as I had done.

The final meetings began on Wednesday night and were to be in Fitchburg, MA, where about 12 churches had come together to bring in revival through Randy. Once again, as Randy asked the approximately 525 assembled how many had heard him speak before, no more than 50 raised their hands. Randy did what he was best at - he totally disarmed them. He very humbly laid a foundation about who he was. He talked about how God sovereignly used him, a very ordinary guy, but one who has dedicated himself to being a "God chaser." As he poked fun at his manner and speech, they fell in love with him.

Friday was the final night. It had been a great three days of meetings. Over the last 16 months I had written many reports on these meetings, and it showed this night. His message was once again on "Pressing In." He would often begin the message by throwing some of his products to the congregation, but for the last one he would say, "Who wants this one? It's free to anyone who wants it, you can have it, it's free!" Many wanted to come forward and get it because he wasn't throwing it like the others, but they held back. Almost always, the person who finally got it wasn't the one who was closest, but the one that was the boldest. Well, a lot of people had apparently read my reports of this phenomenon. Several just charged at Randy as soon as he said the above, and one man took it from him forcefully.

ANGELS AND FEATHERS

I had tried to be careful in writing these reports, and as I was reviewing them for this book, I noticed I had omitted this point. At that time I don't know that everyone was ready for so much talk about angels, but now it seems to be more common. One time I had caught some flak for saying in a report that "William Branham was one of the most anointed men for healing ever," so, we figured, "let's not rock the boat with talk about angels to people who weren't there at the meetings to understand the context of the discussion." On that night in Fitchburg, just as Randy was beginning his teaching, a feather began to fall. Bill Johnson, who had been doing the morning teaching sessions, caught it, put it in Randy's wallet and handed it back to him. When Randy placed it in his back pocket, he immediately got "drunk." That was something I had only seen about three times in all the time I had traveled with him. He actually had to toss his wallet back over for Bill to keep while he spoke.

We had another person get truly "blasted' in these meetings and it began to radically change his life. Dennis McCormick was in the meetings and at different times Randy and I prayed and prophesied over him. It so impacted him that he volunteered to drive Carol and I to pick up a rental car, since we were staying over the next few days before returning home. He was just desperate to talk about what had happened to him, and where he would go from there. He was some sort of software engineer, but he was effectively ruined for normal life after this. It further escalated in the next few years as he went on several trips with Randy and the teams he was taking to foreign countries. Dennis saw many creative miracles and would later become one of Randy's older interns. We felt privileged to have spoken over him, to have prayed for him and ignite his fire and passion.

WE'RE INVITED THE ENEMY RISES, BUT WE'RE STILL STANDING

We had planned on taking the weekend to see a little of New England before returning to California, but now there was a change of plans. The pastor, Daryl Nicolete, who was the lead pastor in putting on this conference, had asked us to speak at his church Sunday. God gave Carol a message immediately, which made us think we God might have been in on all this, so we accepted. After wrapping up all the details of the meetings, and seeing Randy and the team off to their homes, attack, confusion, and intimidation immediately came in. Carol lost confidence in her message and I felt intimidated. These people had just spent three days under the ministry and teaching of Randy Clark and Bill Johnson. Plus, Bill, being Daryl's brother-in-law, had been to his church several times. I had to keep in focus that we **are** the message - that message that God really can use "little ole me," no matter what kind of a background we come from, what the circumstances are, and that each of us plays a part in God's Kingdom.

By Sunday morning, the enemy had taken his shot at us and we were still standing. God had clarified our message of "being hungry" and wanting us to be "filled to spill." Carol knew she was to talk about the parable in Luke 14:16 about the banquet, and then I was to tell some stories of people we had met who were "spillin'." When Daryl made the announcements before we spoke, that after the service many were going to the convalescent home to serve and minister, we knew God had given us a confirming message. It was just a great morning, as we finished our mini-vacation in New England.

A RESOURCE TEAM OUT OF SAN DIEGO

On Monday we returned to San Diego to celebrate Thanksgiving, having moved on in our ministry. We were facing the unknown, but we were excited. We had one meeting set up - what more could you want. It was a start, and that's all we needed to be encouraged. As we returned home, we were soon given the opportunity to minister in several other churches in January. Also, Randy's schedule was such that he would be coming to California several times in February and March of 2000, giving us the opportunity to train in those churches prior to his coming. That, actually, was a key to our getting started. We were able to meet and connect with many other churches, and we've been traveling and ministering since then.

Sixteen months prior to this time, I had been hungry for more of a healing anointing. I had known that I had to get to Vacaville for a week long conference with Randy Clark in June of 1998, even though it made no sense economically. My goal was to be on the ministry team, and to catch an anointing for healing that I could take back to San Diego, to the church I was attending. I was hungry and desperate for "more," and I got so much more than I could have hoped for.

I got to meet Randy, become his "driver" and got invited to travel with him. He was mentoring Ben, and I knew he wasn't mentoring me, that he wasn't grooming me for ministry. I was to help him administratively, but I would have the opportunity to minister alongside him. We never discussed what would be the outcome, but as I traveled and got more involved, it became my hope and desire that perhaps, one day, we would be able to minister as one of his Resource Teams - basically doing what he was doing for the Body of Christ.

Now we had returned to San Diego, taking the training we had learned, and what God had imparted to us, to do renewal meetings and prayer ministry training and equipping. We'd had the chance to join the Global Awakening team and partner with some wonderful and anointed people. We felt honored to be associated with the quality and character of the people in that organization. I had learned so much from Randy. I learned about "pressing in for more," about contending with God for the power to flow through me, about the importance of relationship, and about handling the anointing with character. I was also grateful for the chance to be the "scribe" for those many months and many, many meetings. I had chronicled renewal through those times. Being a history major in college, I know those reports are important for future generations to learn from.

Looking back, I wonder why I wasn't more concerned about how God would use us. Could we really have a ministry? Would we be able to make a difference in people's lives? Would churches really want us to come in to minister in their churches - after all, we weren't Randy. Would God back us up - would we see healings, deliverances, prophecy, the move of the Spirit, etc? Even in the face of all of that, I never was really worried. I just went for it. We immediately saw people get healed and delivered. We prophesied. And, most importantly, we made a difference in people's lives. We have had many people say they were touched by our ministry. A pastor said something we have remembered and clung to - after a weekend of meetings, he said, "We can tell God is with you, that you're anointed. But you're just so *ordinary,* and, you make us believe we can do this too!" That's the nicest thing anyone could say about us. We've seen some incredible things happen, as the power of God has come into our meetings, and is continuing to do so with even more power. Perhaps that's the subject of another book.

I know I've told a lot of stories about people getting healed or being set free. Frankly, I never get bored hearing or telling the stories. Hopefully you're not bored either. The reality is that we in the North American church have become very much like the Israelites. They were constantly reminded to tell the testimonies (Deut 6:17), but they forgot - they didn't tell the stories of his works (Psalm 78:41). We've done the same thing. So, for me, the remembering and the telling of the testimonies is critical to feed myself with the things God **is** doing and **has** done, so I don't fall into the trap of focusing on what He **hasn't** done.

I, and many others, believe we have entered into the greatest move of God since Pentecost. We are going to see and be part of the things generations before have longed to see. I pray that this story of how Carol and I moved into this renewal and what it was like in those early days has been an encouragement to you. I often say this when speaking, and I say it to you again. Many of you will have a revelation as you hear this story, and this is what you'll say: "If God can use him, I *know* He can use me!" Be "filled to spill" and bring Heaven to earth everywhere you go. I charge you to be "armed and dangerous, 24/7, without being weird!" Take the love and power of God and begin to make a difference in your community. May you be richly blessed on this incredible journey of "thy Kingdom come, thy will be done, on earth as it is in Heaven."

ABOUT THE AUTHOR

Bill and Carol Dew believe every follower of Christ is to heal the sick, cleanse the lepers, raise the dead and cast out demons, and they are on a mission to see this happen. Working with churches, apostolic networks, other ministries, and ministry schools, they are equipping believers to be who Jesus said they could be and do what He said they could do.

As they teach and impart through the laying on of hands, believers begin to move in greater power and confidence, becoming naturally supernatural everywhere they go, twenty-four/seven. They are reproducing the miracle-working ministry of Jesus in Christians and helping them obey His command to "Go and make disciples of all nations...teaching them to obey everything I have commanded you."

Bill was a successful commercial real estate agent and Carol a content housewife and mother until God interrupted their comfortable lives. Carol received a call into ministry in 1981. She graduated from Fuller Theological Seminary with an MDiv in 1988 and became an ordained Presbyterian pastor. God arrested Bill in 1992 and transformed him from a nominal Christian into a passionate, Spirit-filled believer with a call to the healing ministry. Bill left the business world and became sold-out for God. Their marriage and ministry were radically changed during a three week stay at the Toronto Airport Christian Fellowship in 1996, and life has been an incredible adventure ever since.

Bill traveled full-time with Randy Clark from August 1998 through November, 1999. During that time he, and Carol who joined him on many of those trips, both received a powerful anointing for healing and an anointing to impart it to others. Carol is trained as an Elijah House prayer counselor and is anointed in inner healing.

Bill and Carol have ministered in many denominational and non-denominational churches and groups throughout the United States and internationally. Home for Bill and Carol is San Diego, CA. They have been married since 1969 and have one grown daughter.

For more information on
Dewnamis Ministries

go to

www.dewnamis.com